Do Christians Know How to Be Spiritual?

The rise of New Spirituality, and the mission of the Church

JOHN DRANE

DARTON · LONGMAN + TODD

First published in 2005 by
Darton, Longman and Todd Ltd
1 Spencer Court
140-142 Wandsworth High Street
London SW18 4JJ

ISBN 0 232 52632 X

A catalogue record for this book is available from the British Library.

Designed by Sandie Boccacci
Phototypeset by IntypeLibra Ltd

Printed and bound in Great Britain by
The Cromwell Press, Trowbridge, Wiltshire

Contents

Foreword

Founded in 1974, the London Lectures in Contemporary Christianity aim to expound some aspect of historical Christianity, to relate it to a contemporary issue in the church or the world, to be scholarly in content yet popular in appeal and presentation and to present each topic in such a way as to be of interest to people who are not Christians.

It is hard to see how these aims could have been more fully met than by John Drane's lectures in 2004, which explored new expressions of spirituality and a Christian response and which are presented in this volume. John's wisdom, learning and practical experience have been used to good effect in dealing with a topic of immense significance as Western humanity asks profound questions about meaning and identity. If Christian mission is to make any impact it cannot ignore these issues.

The lectures are organised by the London Lectures Trust which was established as a charity in 1994. The committee represents several evangelical organisations and we owe a great debt to Penny Boshoff, the Honorary Administrator, who carries the major burden and who did a superb job of organising this series.

In recent years the lectures have been published by Inter-Varsity Press, an arrangement which has served us well and to which we shall revert in future years. Given the lecturer's existing relationship with Darton, Longman and Todd, and their reputation for publishing in this area, it was agreed that the lectures for this year should be published by them and it has been a privilege to work with them. CDs and audio tapes can be obtained from ICC, Silverdale Road, Eastbourne BN20 7AB. For further details of future lectures please contact Penny Boshoff, The London Lectures Trust Office, 36 Copperfields, Kemsing, Kent TN15 6QG.

John Grayston
Chair, London Lectures Committee

Preface

I suppose most people have a handful of experiences in life that fall into the category of 'things I shall never forget'. One of my most unforgettable occasions was back in 1990, at a dinner party where the other main guest was the leader of one of Britain's major Christian denominations. Like many clergymen of his generation, he oozed that mixture of intellectual pretension and greasy unctuousness that has so often been caricatured in the media as being the very essence of Christian leadership. By way of polite conversation, he asked me about my current interests, no doubt expecting that I would direct him to some obscure Bible verse or abstruse topic of classic theological discourse. But it so happened that only a few weeks previously I had been in California doing research for a book on what we all then called 'the New Age'. In the course of my visit, I had interviewed many therapists and spiritual advisers who were definitely towards the 'wacky' end of alternative spirituality, including some of the leading lights in the movement. So it was natural for me to respond to this polite expression of interest by describing some of the experiences I had had, and venturing the opinion that this burgeoning interest in the spiritual was likely to be one of the most important subjects for any Christian leader to know about – whether in the Church or (as I was at the time) in the academy. As he listened to what I had to say, his entire body language changed and it was obvious that he could hardly believe what he was hearing. By the end of the evening, I was left in no doubt that my reputation as an up-and-coming theologian had been well and truly destroyed, because serious people did not concern themselves with such trivia. At the time, I hardly knew whether to be more embarrassed for him or for my long-suffering hosts, who had done their best to create a pleasant atmosphere but were forced to spend much of the evening listening to a lecture on what 'real' theologians were supposed to do. Somewhat surprisingly, perhaps, I have no recollection of being embarrassed for myself, nor did it occur to me that I should consider reordering the future course of my life in order to become more conventional.

Church leaders do not react that way today. Throughout the intervening fifteen years, active involvement in all forms of Christian activity has been in significant decline, while the concerns represented by the 'new age' movement of the early 1990s have moved from the counter-culture onto centre-stage, and to one degree or another have been incorporated into the mainstream world view of people throughout the Western world. The correlation between these two trends can be overstated, and it is arguable that the Church's decline owes as much to its own internal bickering as it does to overt competition from other spiritualities. Nevertheless, common sense suggests that the decline of the Church and the rising popularity of a more loosely defined 'spirituality' cannot be entirely unrelated to one another.

The contents of this book were first delivered as the London Lectures in Contemporary Christianity in 2004, and the mere fact that the London Lectures Trust invited me to speak on this topic is itself a sign of how much things have changed. It was also, for me, a sign that (contrary to the dire predictions offered to me back in 1990) I had not wasted my life in the meantime, and I am grateful to the trustees of the London Lectures for their affirmation and the confidence they placed in me. I was also encouraged by the audiences that turned up over four consecutive weeks in November 2004, not only by the significant numbers in which they came, but also by the warm reception that was given to what I said. It seemed that the more provocative I was, the more they loved it, and it was a real pleasure to engage with people who genuinely wanted to learn more about the topic, and who came with open minds and (whether Christian or not) a desire to know what God might be saying to us all at this point in history. In writing these lectures up for publication, I have chosen to stick very closely to what was actually said at the time. The only thing I have changed is the overall title (the lectures were on 'Spirituality, Christianity, and the Future of the World', which may have been somewhat pretentious and was certainly too long-winded to become the title of a book). But apart from that,

I have preserved the original outline (there were four lectures, and there are four chapters here), and in some places I have retained the conversational style of the spoken word. Time and again I came across topics that could have been expanded in multiple ways, but I made a deliberate choice not to allow the book to deviate too far from its origins, partly because it would have increased its size, but also because I am in the process of writing the sequel to my previous book *The McDonaldization of the Church*, and many of these issues will be given further consideration there.

I was particularly relieved to have receptive audiences for the lectures, as I was in the midst of what turned out to be one of the most stressful periods of my entire life. When I accepted the invitation to give the lectures, I had a well-paid senior position in a university, where I had assumed I would stay for the next ten years or so, or even until retirement. By the time the lectures came around, I had resigned from that position without having any obvious alternative employment, and if I were being honest I think that travelling to London to fulfil my commitment was just about the last thing I wanted to do. In the event, though, it turned out to be exactly the right thing. The hospitality and friendship extended to me and my wife Olive by the staff and students of Spurgeon's College, where we stayed throughout the month, was intellectually satisfying and personally enriching for us both in a way that restored some of our trust in human nature. The experience of being part of that vibrant faith community (where 'community' was as important as 'faith') drew my attention to the fact that, throughout the time when I had been trying to decide whether I should leave the academy, I had actually been wrestling with matters that are themselves at the heart of today's concern for a more holistic 'spiritual' way of being: values such as trust, honesty, integrity, acceptance, and openness.

I had a similarly positive – if more attenuated – experience during the writing of this book, when I had the opportunity to present some of my ideas in a public lecture at Trinity College, Dublin. The warm response I received on that occasion, from a completely different sort of audience, encouraged me to believe that what I have to say is relevant for Christians of all traditions, and also helped to sharpen up some of the proposals made in the final chapter here, which had been offered in a more muted form in the original London Lectures.

Finally, I must thank those who facilitated the London Lectures: John Grayston and Penny Boshoff who did much of the hard work to make them happen, and Gospatric Home, Peter Graystone and Brian Draper who each chaired one of the lectures. And last, but not least, let me mention the founder of this annual series, John Stott, who not only encouraged me during the time of my preparation but also attended and prayed for and with me. It is in a spirit of such prayerfulness that I have continued to create this book from the lectures. There is a lot of challenging stuff in here, some of which I am still working through in my own thinking and spiritual practice. But it is born out of a lifelong commitment to following Jesus Christ, and a concern to share the good news of what I have discovered with others who are intentionally searching for a spiritual dimension to life. I commend it to my readers with confidence that, while I will have got some things wrong, many more things will be pointing in the right direction. In the words of the poem 'He Wishes for the Cloths of Heaven' by W.B. Yeats,

> I have spread my dreams under your feet;
> Tread softly because you tread on my dreams.[1]

John Drane
Easter Day 2005

1 From 'Religion' to 'Spirituality'

Twenty years ago, the word would have been all but unknown to the vast majority of people in Western cultures. It was in the dictionary, of course, and in certain religious circles some individuals did use it. But for the average person in Europe, if 'spirituality' had any meaning at all, it would have invoked images of a way of life that belonged to past history, perhaps represented by ancient buildings and religious monuments, along with traditional stories of the saints of a bygone era. Americans might have been a little more familiar with the terminology, especially those who had come into contact with the Californian version of the 1960s' revolution, with its emphasis on flower power and self-discovery. But even in the US, most people who were not personally involved in these movements would have been more likely to identify 'spirituality' with various fringe groups that claimed to receive messages from some other world, such as Theosophy, or the Spiritualist Church, or with new religions such as Mormonism or Christian Science. The average person on both sides of the Atlantic would certainly not have embraced 'spirituality' as part of their everyday experience – nor would being 'spiritual' have been widely regarded as something to aspire to.

Now, at the beginning of the twenty-first century, things are completely different. Putting the word 'spirituality' into a web search engine comes up with more than fifteen million results. Though we might all have our own definitions of what we think it is, the notion of 'spirituality', or of 'being spiritual' is part and parcel of everyday life. Adverts try to sell everything from food to jewellery, movies, vacations, cosmetics, education, and much more besides – on the basis that these products will enhance a person's 'spirituality'. But this is far more than just an advertising gimmick, for there has been an exponential growth in the numbers of individuals and organizations that offer more overtly 'spiritual' goods and services that may look as if they have some connection with traditional religious beliefs, while at the same time being completely different from them. In a random survey of a single recent issue of *The Whole Person* (a monthly calendar of 'spiritual events'), adverts for retreat centres jostle for position alongside 'spiritual' dentists (who will fill your teeth with crystals, long believed to have special healing powers), courses on life purpose coaching, the Kabbalah, relationship counselling, pre-natal attunement, rebirthing and past-life regression, as well as more everyday things like restaurants and car dealers. One therapist (Kenny Rich) asks, 'Would you like to become God?' – to which he responds, 'If you do, it's in your birth chart how to do it, and I can tell you how, because that's my job'. He even offers a money-back guarantee, telling readers,

> I have no formal fees . . . you send me a check, or you don't, cause if you didn't like the reading, and don't think that I delivered what I promised, and didn't tell you how to become the God of your own life, and how to solve all of your problems, and how to create everything you want, I wouldn't want you to pay anyway, but if I did deliver what I promised, you owe me more than money could ever pay, but you get to send me a check, and we'll call it even.[1]

Origins

It is tempting to dismiss all this as the self-centred indulgence of Western people with too much time and money on their hands, and not enough concern for the rest of the world. But there is more to it than that. For what we are seeing today has authentic roots in historic Western culture, particularly in the USA, but also in Britain and Europe more generally. Americans have always been fascinated by the spiritual, partly because many more of them have some living connection to traditional faith communities in churches and synagogues than is now the case in Europe – but also because 'spirituality' in various guises has been a significant influence in establishing the identity of a nation whose origins lay in other countries and cultures. It was a conscious spiritual motivation that led to the Pilgrims leaving Europe and establishing a new life for themselves at Plimoth Plantation, and through them the Puritans had a strong influence right from the start. Much later, though, at the emergence of the modern nation, 'spirituality' of a different type fascinated many of the founding fathers – this time an interest in the sort of arcane folklore and ancient mythology that is still represented by the mystical symbols that are inscribed on the back of every dollar bill. The nineteenth century saw the development of several home-grown American religious movements, all of them based on belief in metaphysical realities, and many of them offering a personal connection with the transcendent either through the stories of their founders or by direct experience of the paranormal. Encounters with angels featured strongly in the life of Ellen G. White (1827–1915), founder of the Seventh Day Adventist Church. The Church of Jesus Christ of Latter Day Saints (Mormons) came to birth when one of her near-contemporaries, Joseph Smith (1805–44), published *The Book of Mormon* in 1830 – a book that he believed had originally been inscribed on golden plates, which were then hidden near Palmyra, in the state of New York, and whose secret location was revealed to him by Moroni, an angelic being from the New World.

Other religious teachers of the time included Mary Baker Eddy (1821–1910), founder of Christian Science, and Ralph Waldo Emerson (1803–82), one-time Congregationalist minister who first became a Unitarian before eventually designating himself as a 'transcendentalist' minister. Emerson was especially influenced by his discovery of the teachings of the classic Indian text, the *Bhagavad Gita*, and fascination with Indian spirituality also dominated the thinking of other significant figures of the time, most notably Helena Blavatsky (1831–91) who in 1875 was one of the founders of the Theosophical Society. Her particular claim to fame was the ability to receive messages from what she called 'Masters of Wisdom', or 'Ascended Masters', individuals who had gone through many reincarnations and as a consequence had acquired considerably more wisdom about the nature of things than those who were still alive. Just a few years earlier, the possibility of receiving messages from beings in other worlds had attracted public attention through events in Hydesville NY, home of John and Margaret Fox and their two daughters, Margaret and Kate. After hearing a series of unusual banging noises in the wall of their farm cottage, the family decided on 31 March 1848 to challenge whoever was making them to identify themselves. Something – or someone – responded to their challenge, claiming to be the spirit of a person murdered there long before. This disembodied spirit also appeared to have uncanny knowledge of everyday events in the Foxes' own lives. It knew the number and ages of all John and Margaret's children, including some who had lived for only a short time. Within eighteen months, the two daughters had become celebrities, and following the publicity given to their story, contacting the spirits of the dead became something of an obsession, in Britain as well as America.

Interest in such matters was not altogether a new thing in Europe. Two centuries before, Baron Emanuel Swedenborg (1688–1772) had testified to similarly unusual experiences, which he described in the preface to his eight-volume *Arcana Coelestia*, written in Latin between 1749 and 1756, as an experience of being 'constantly and uninterruptedly in company with spirits and angels, hearing them speak and in turn speaking with them'. The same aspirations also surfaced in the work of some well-known British writers of the time, particularly in the poetry of Percy Shelley (1792–1822), William Wordsworth (1770–1850), Alfred Tennyson (1809–92), and the romantic visionary William Blake (1757–1827). In his poem 'Timbuctoo', written in 1829, Tennyson described how

> . . . other things talking in unknown tongues,
> And notes of busy life in distant worlds
> Beat like a far wave on my anxious ear.

Like his younger contemporary W.B. Yeats (1865–1939), Tennyson was a great admirer of Blavatsky's Theosophical Society. Even scientists could be fascinated by such possibilities. Thomas Edison (1847–1931), for example, was fascinated by mystical possibilities, as also was Lord Kelvin (1824–1907), who in his 1871 presidential address to the British Association for the

Advancement of Science spoke in these terms of the origins of life itself:

> because we all confidently believe that there are at present, and have been from time immemorial, many worlds of life besides our own, we must regard it as probable in the highest degree that there are countless seed-bearing meteoric stones moving about through space . . . The hypothesis that life originated on this earth through moss-grown fragments from the ruins of another world may seem wild and visionary; all I maintain is that it is not unscientific.

This sort of speculative spirituality continued into the early twentieth century, being especially influential in aristocratic circles. It was among such people that Arthur Waite produced what came to be the definitive form of the Tarot, which has turned out to be one of the most popular spiritual tools of the twenty-first century.[2] Not long after, the enormous death toll of the First World War inspired many others to take an interest in such esoteric matters – either to discover what had happened to lost loved ones, or to search for a way of understanding the world that would both avoid and correct what were increasingly seen as the undesirable consequences of a scientific and industrial establishment that had apparently lost all sense of values. Throughout the middle years of the twentieth century, a more rational and materialist world view prevailed, which coincided with serious decline in the traditional sources of spiritual wisdom (the churches), especially in Europe. But with the cultural upheaval of the 1960s, a fascination for spirituality once again emerged onto the popular agenda. At first, it was a novelty reserved for those with enough time and money to follow those celebrities who were travelling to India and other Asian destinations in search of spiritual insights. But a growing awareness of other cultures, ancient as well as contemporary, and a realization that Western ways of being had not delivered the peace and security that they promised, opened up the spiritual search to increasing numbers of people so that by the end of the twentieth century 'spirituality' was everywhere. It was even being studied by serious academics, and had been given a name: the New Age.

Definitions

It is hard enough even to describe the pastiche of attitudes and interests represented by what has been called the New Age, without trying to analyse it or understand its significance. Most outside observers have tended to be somewhat negative about it all. Sociology professor Steve Bruce regards it as almost entirely irrelevant for understanding contemporary culture,[3] while religion professor Paul Heelas characterizes it as a self-centred, self-indulgent movement,[4] and Jeremy Carrette and Richard King describe it as 'a new cultural addiction' that is damaging to both individuals and societies.[5] Walter Truett Anderson, writing in a more journalistic vein, dismisses the current interest in 'spirituality' as a 'scene of goofy cults and fuzzy spirituality', 'a vast fountain of trivialization, commercialization, sloppy thinking, and general smarminess' – and even those with some personal sympathy for it find themselves hard pressed to disagree with his proposition that it is best described as an 'amorphous subculture'.[6] In trying to pin 'New Age' down more precisely, Denise Cush, for example, offers a minimalist understanding of the phenomenon as 'a cluster of related ideas, teachings and groups, not altogether coherent, most of which would identify with this title'[7] – a way of 'defining' it which only serves to highlight the difficulty of doing so. This lack of clarity is a major reason why I wish to propose here an altogether different paradigm for understanding contemporary spirituality.

New Age and New Spirituality

The terminology itself is part of the problem, for the mere act of applying a label to something tends to suggest that it is a more fixed phenomenon than is actually the case. The term 'New Age' came to prominence in California in the mid-1980s, though the notion of a coming 'new age' of radical transformation for the world and its people can be traced at least as far back as the various nineteenth-century movements already mentioned, and some writers claim that it is of even more ancient origin. In the 1960s, the concept of 'the Age of Aquarius' was introduced to Western audiences through the rock musical *Hair* whose theme song declared 'This is the Age of Aquarius', which it further defined as 'the age of the mind's true liberation'. The roots of this way of speaking can be found in various psychological theories that had their origins in the middle years of the twentieth century, and which had been connected with pre-existing esoteric religious and mystical traditions through the work of academics and other researchers who gathered at the Esalen Institute in Big Sur, California. But the notion of an 'Age of Aquarius' originated in astrological speculations related to the signs of the zodiac, according to which the whole of human history can be divided into periods of 1260 years. On this reckoning we are currently at the end of the Age of Pisces and on the verge of the dawning of the Age of Aquarius. Unlike the ages which have gone immediately before, this 'new age' will be characterized by peace, wholeness, and harmony – for people, and ultimately for the whole cosmos. In the process, we are destined to realize that we are not at the mercy of external, objective forces but that the only real energy is within ourselves and the only reality we experience is what we create ourselves. As Marilyn Ferguson expressed it in one of the classic expositions of this world view:

> The paradigm of the Aquarian conspiracy sees humankind embedded in nature. It promotes the autonomous individual in a decentralized society. It sees us as stewards of our resources, inner and outer. It says that we are not victims, not pawns, not limited by conditions and conditioning.[8]

The taxonomy of different astrological ages is still to be found, and is occasionally used as a way of comparing and contrasting the rise of 'spirituality' and the demise of 'religion' (by equating Pisces, the fish, with the age of Christianity, and Aquarius, the water bearer, with the emerging culture). But the majority of people who are interested in 'spirituality' today would not espouse that world view, which is one more reason why we need to question the appropriateness of continuing to use the terminology of 'new age' to describing their concerns.

Another reason for re-examining the way we describe the phenomenon of contemporary spirituality is that many who once would have applied the term 'New Age' to themselves are now increasingly seeking to distance themselves from it. There is a widely held perception that it has come to be unhelpfully identified with ideas and practices that are, at best, eccentric and bizarre. In her history of the Findhorn Foundation, Carol Riddell makes this point very strongly:

> We are now a little wary of this description, which was once eagerly embraced by the Findhorn Community, because in popular thought it has become connected with the sensation seekers . . . whose interest lies less in seeking spiritual transformation than in dabbling in the occult, or in practising classical capitalist entrepreneurship on the naïve.[9]

There can be no doubt that these protests are fully justified. Though Carrette and King may be overstating the case with their claim that the rise of popular spirituality is part of some worldwide conspiracy by multinational corporations, the term 'New Age' has certainly been hijacked by commercial interests. In the process, it has been reduced to a collection of self-serving potions and simplistic nostrums that at best are valueless to the serious spiritual searcher,[10] and might even be damaging to more vulnerable individuals who imagine there can be a quick-fix solution for dysfunctional relationships and personality disorders.

Adherents of any particular world view do not always provide the most useful words with which to describe their activities: understandably, the self-descriptions of devotees (emic descriptions) tend to evoke positive images. To reflect on a phenomenon dispassionately, a description from outside (etic description) can not only be more neutral, but can also shed light on aspects that might otherwise pass unnoticed. In this respect, whether applied emically or etically, the term 'New Age' now carries so much baggage that it is no longer serviceable. I have in the past used this terminology myself,[11] but I will not use it here, preferring instead to speak of 'New Spirituality'. Not only does this have the advantage of being a more neutral, descriptive term, but it also affirms the element of serious search for meaning and purpose that has always been at the heart of this mystical strand of Western culture. Its use is also intended to imply that what is now happening is no longer the minority interest of unrepresentative groups of oddballs on the fringes of mainstream culture, but is in important respects central to the self-understanding of Western society today. Another reason for preferring the term 'New Spirituality' is the simple fact that the way in which the notion of the spiritual is now utilized in the culture is very diverse and eclectic, as we shall see in the next chapter, and in significant ways has moved away from the arcane topics associated with 'New Age' ideas and practices. The interests represented by what has hitherto been called 'New Age' are undoubtedly a part of what I am describing here as New Spirituality, but not all New Spirituality would qualify as 'New Age'.

Religion, spirituality, and institutions

That may sound like a clumsy way of expressing it, but identifying appropriate terminology is actually the easy part of the discussion. The bigger challenge is what we mean by it. What, exactly, is 'spirituality'? In one sense, that is a silly question, because in and of themselves words have no intrinsic or absolute meaning: their meaning is determined by the context in which they are used. Exploring how a particular word has been used historically can be enlightening up to a point, but ultimately the most important thing is the meaning we attach to it today.[12] When we look to the way in which the term 'spirituality' is now being used, one thing stands out above all others: it is used less to describe what a particular belief system, therapy, or experience *is* and more to describe what it *is not*. In particular, 'spirituality' is not 'religion'. 'Religion' itself, of course, is another slippery word, and historically one can say that in the past religion and spirituality have been virtually indistinguishable. There is a lot to be said for Carrette and King's argument that 'religion' as a discrete category of human existence is somewhat meaningless, because a person's beliefs and world view have always been inseparable from their cultural context.[13] But since we are here dealing with a popular view of the matter, as it might be perceived not by informed academics but by the average person, it is not at all inappropriate that we should at least begin with the sort of widely held view that might be encountered in everyday life, even if it might later be necessary to question or qualify it. Nowadays, 'religion' tends to be used to describe some externally imposed world view and set of practices, requiring conformity on the part of those who engage in it, backed up by narrow-minded attitudes based on dogmatic understandings of the meaning of everything – all of this enforced by hierarchical structures that are riddled with hypocrisy and self-serving in a way that exploits others and prevents them reaching their full potential as human beings (which is an intrinsic part of the package because, if we were to be fully empowered, we would in turn challenge the hierarchies who run religions). 'Spirituality' has emerged as the preferred term to describe the opposite of these things. It is the agent through which we might reach our full potential as human beings, and to be considered 'spiritual' an idea or attitude needs to come across as promoting wholeness and healing – of ourselves, of society, and ultimately of the entire cosmos.[14] As Rodney Clapp puts it, 'spirituality' is 'a word we turn to in preference to certain other, less appealing alternatives',[15] and which 'permits us to name [our aspirations for meaning, purpose and identity in life] while not implying that we are prudish or conformist or pretentious or naïve.'[16] James Gollnick offers a slightly more specific account of the term as 'a quest for the sacred involving a person's identity, values and worldview'.[17]

It is not difficult to understand how this shift of meaning has occurred, so that 'religion' has come to be regarded as a bad thing and 'spirituality' as its opposite. Millions of people who have never heard of the militaristic excesses of religions through the ages will forever associate 'religion' (in this case, a certain form of Islam) with the events of September 11, 2001, while the subsequent military adventures led by the US and its allies appear to have been overtly inspired by the beliefs of Christians, especially those who buy into an apocalyptic version of the faith that is looking for the last great battle of Armageddon to take place in the Middle East and which regards Western politicians as having a central part to play in that drama.[18] In the case of Christianity, there is the further fact that it has been such an integral part of Western culture for the last thousand years and more that the average person finds it all but impossible to disentangle Christian beliefs and values from the inherited values of the wider culture. In this frame of reference, the belief that religion is a bad thing is an intrinsic aspect of the growing consensus that the scientific and materialist world view on which Western society has been based for the last five hundred years or so has failed to deliver on its promises. The great Enlightenment vision of a better world for everyone has simply not come to pass. Not only has the fundamental human predicament not improved, but as the twentieth century progressed things actually got worse, and the trend has continued into the twenty-first century. What is more, the increasing pace of change, and the accompanying difficulties of keeping up with it, are affecting people everywhere – in the workplace and the family, as well as on the global and international scene. Who in the early 1980s would have believed that by the end of that decade Communism could have collapsed so totally in eastern Europe – and done so almost literally overnight? Or that in the light of subsequent events in more recent years, the cold war of the 1960s and 1970s would look like a time of unparalleled safety and security? Change is nothing new, but in previous generations things tended to change slowly, which meant people could adapt with relative ease as part of a naturally evolving process. The faster the pace of change, the more difficult it is to handle, and in many instances the solutions to today's problems are likely to be redundant long before they can be implemented. The world is moving on all the time, which means we are likely to fall further and further behind in coping with things. No wonder that these increasing pressures are demanding a reappraisal of some of the most basic questions of all. Matters that our grandparents thought had been settled for all time are now up for debate again – questions about the world and its systems, about life and its meaning, about people and their relationships, about values and religion. In general, we are becoming less and less satisfied with the traditional answers that are handed down to us, whether from science or religion.

Science and technology have produced many benefits, which it would be impossible – and foolish – to deny. Modern medical science must surely have improved the lifestyle of most of us, and the development of efficient worldwide transportation systems has done much to open our eyes to the global dimensions of our own lives. But the course of progress has not run smoothly. At the end of the nineteenth century, it was confidently believed that as evolution progressed the human race would be improving all the time. It is impossible to believe that any more. The senseless carnage of the First World War and the industrialized death camps set up by the Nazis were not isolated shameful episodes. On the contrary, they turned out to be typical of international relationships throughout the twentieth century, which witnessed more bloody conflicts than any other comparable period in the whole of history. The opening years of the twenty-first century brought more of the same. People are more fearful today than at any time in recent history – whether of terrorist attacks in the wake of 9/11, or of uncontrollable natural forces following the tsunami disaster that hit parts of Asia at the end of 2004. Of course, scientific and technological progress is not in itself a bad thing. Who could have foreseen that so many inventive discoveries would be used to develop ever more terrifying ways of annihilating people? Who could have imagined that improving standards of health care, leading to longer life expectancy and falling rates of infant mortality, would enable the world's population to increase to the point where many nations are constantly balanced on a knife edge between survival and extinction? Who could have predicted that the efficient use of fertilizers and pesticides to produce more food for this expanding population would lead to the pollution of the world's water, one of the most precious resources of all? How could anyone have guessed that the development of modern transportation systems, and the fuels used to operate them, would lead to the depletion of the ozone layer, with its evident results in unpredictable climatic change?

Over and above the insecurities generated by these concerns, an enormous number of people have, for one reason or another, lost faith in their institutions, and conclude that the remaining structures are concerned mainly for their own survival and welfare as institutions. Mistrust and cynicism are the order of the day. Physicians, with their strict Hippocratic oath and commitment to other people's welfare, were once highly regarded as the least corruptible profession of all. Today they are often viewed with suspicion as people with more interest in patient hours and covering their overheads than in the health and welfare of those whom they treat. Even those patients who are not quite so cynical still find themselves drawn to alternative therapies and holistic health techniques, simply because the professional medic no longer has enough time to deal adequately with the needs of every single patient. Trust in politicians is also at an all-time low, not to mention the disdain with which accountants are held in the wake of recent scandals. Religion fares no better, especially Christianity, which is seen as part and parcel of the Western establishment and is therefore subjected to the same suspicions as other institutions. Many people have come to believe that whatever spiritual reality the churches may once have had, it has been siphoned off or suppressed in the interests of the ecclesiastical power structures, and that the professional clergy are so concerned with keeping the machinery going and maintaining their own vested interests in control and position that they too have lost touch with any kind of movement of the spirit. Even those who are sympathetic to the Church are no longer able to deny the reality of such opinions. Anglican researcher George Lings is not being cynical, but simply telling it the way it is when he writes that for many people:

> Church stands for internal bickering over issues no one else cares about, inconsistent lives that make claims in ridiculous words, led by people who don't know what they believe and are probably to be distrusted with other people's children.[19]

There is a widespread feeling that Western institutions in general have denied their core values, by being more concerned about structures than people. If the core values of Christian faith have also been marginalized as the Church becomes ever more McDonaldized,[20] then the obvious conclusion to be drawn by individuals looking for meaning and purpose in their lives is that those values are unlikely to be located in the mainstream establishment, but will be found on the fringes – whether in individualistic forms of Christianity or in the transformational therapies offered by the New Spirituality. The 'Christianity without

Religion' movement, based in the Canary Islands, speaks for many when its publicity warns: 'You owe it to your God to stay away from organized institutionalized man-made religion', and then continues, 'Empty prayer in empty churches is noise . . .', urging readers, 'You can become a living church without religion, so act now – serve God, not man!'

Whether all this is a wholly accurate analysis of Western culture is not our concern just now. The fact is that enough people feel this way for it to have had a significant impact on their attitudes toward traditional religious faith. For that reason, it affects the places in which it seems reasonable to search for meaning and identity in the context of a world that has apparently lost its way. Few would now deny that we have been unable to change or improve the world even by our own best efforts. The dream that inspired our forebears has turned to a nightmare. But people still aspire to a better life, in which we can live in harmony with one another, at peace with our planet, and in tune with ourselves. The longing for 'spiritual' purpose is deeply rooted in the human heart, and if traditional Western materialist routes to personal fulfilment and transformation are blocked, it is natural to conclude that we must have been looking in the wrong place.[21]

Spirituality and cultural change

If we could bring back some of the leading intellectuals of previous generations, they would be amazed at the intense interest in spiritual affairs that is now in evidence not only in Western cultures, but more or less throughout the world. It was back in 1882 that Friedrich Nietzsche (1844–1900) famously declared that 'God is dead'[22] by which he meant that humans could no longer believe in a cosmic order beyond the here and now. Yet 'God' – by various definitions and in diverse manifestations – is not only very much alive, but is apparently playing an ever more significant role not only in the private lives of individuals but also in world affairs. Like other rationalists of his day – Marx, Freud, Feuerbach, and others – Nietzsche regarded the notion of 'God' as little more than a hangover from a pre-scientific past. It was a construct created by people in the effort to project order and meaning onto a universe that is ultimately meaningless.

With increasing levels of education, and the general demystifying of the universe through scientific endeavour, he assumed that 'God' must be destined to disappear altogether as humankind progressed and came of age in a materialist universe. For much of the twentieth century, it looked as if such a prognosis might be correct, and some social commentators still believe it is. The title of a book by sociologist Steve Bruce conveys its own message: *God is Dead* – and there can be no denying that involvement in anything 'religious', specifically the Church, has been in steady decline throughout Europe for the last hundred years, and accelerated during the final decade of the last century.[23] That decline still continues, and those Christians who think about such things are now sounding serious alarm bells. Peter Brierley projects a bleak future for Christianity in England (and the same can be said for the rest of the UK, not to mention much of Europe):

> The numbers . . . show a haemorrhage akin to a burst artery. The country is littered with people who used to go to church but no longer do. We could well bleed to death. The tide is running out. At the present rate of change we are one generation from extinction.[24]

Paradoxically, this is by no means the whole picture. The results of the 2001 UK census surprised everyone when it was revealed that some 71.8 per cent of the entire UK population chose to describe themselves as 'Christian'.[25] The significance of this figure is of course open to many different possible understandings, and the way in which the questions were framed (at least for England and Wales) meant that some degree of ambiguity was built in from the start.[26] Even on a minimalist interpretation, though, it demonstrated that faith – even Christian faith – still offers a category which a majority of people find useful when it comes to identifying themselves, whatever they might understand by it, and however they might practise it – or not, as the case may be. Moreover, claiming to be 'of no religion' clearly does not equate with being avowedly atheist, and in view of people's actual practice in times of personal or national crisis it is a reasonable guess that many who say they have no faith will fall into the category of those who see themselves as 'spiritual' rather than 'religious'. Callum Brown may have been overstating the case when he concluded his influential book *The Death of Christian Britain* with the claim that 'Britain is showing the world how religion as we have known it can die'[27] – though it is certainly true that belief is being reconfigured in new ways, and the growth of New Spirituality is part of that.

There has been a good deal of debate as to whether the current interest in 'spirituality' is likely to continue, or whether it represents just a temporary diversion in the otherwise unstoppable onward march of secularization. The secularization hypothesis assumed that wherever scientific and technological insights advanced, commitment to religious faith would disappear, and that the causal connection between the two was so close that the demise of faith would be equivalent to the degree of modernization within the culture. In cultures where the values of modernity prevailed, faith would have a hard time, while in those cultures where religion persisted, modernity would struggle. For decades, this equation seemed unassailable, but the growing influence of religion throughout the world, coupled with the rise of New Spirituality even in European cultures that have ostensibly rejected their traditional religious beliefs, has put serious question marks against this way of understanding cultural change. A significant number of social scientists would now agree with Harvey Cox's opinion that the secularization thesis is 'entirely implausible'.[28]

Until recently, that debate has been conducted on the basis of general impressions, not to mention scholarly hunches – and even at times the personal hang-ups of individual researchers. It has been widely believed that New Spirituality is indeed growing and traditional religion is declining, and that the two trends are intrinsically linked. But little empirical evidence has been available with which to test the hypothesis, nor has it been altogether clear whether there was likely to be a causal connection between the decline of religion and the rise of spirituality in Western culture. That gap in our understanding has recently been addressed in a substantive way through publication of the results of the Kendal Project, a piece of research co-ordinated by Paul Heelas and Linda Woodhead of the University of Lancaster.[29] The aim of the project, which was carried out over a

21-month period between October 2000 and June 2002, was to map the growth of New Spirituality (referred to by Heelas and Woodhead as the 'holistic milieu') in relation to the decline of traditional churchgoing (which they call 'the congregational domain'). Kendal is a small English town of some 28,000 inhabitants, in the county of Cumbria and on the edge of the English Lake District. It is not a pretentious place, nor a recognized destination for self-confessed spiritual searchers, but a semi-rural market town whose population consists of ordinary hard-working families, who find employment in agriculture, tourism, and a handful of small-scale industrial operations. It is the very ordinariness of this place that endues the currents and cross-currents of its spiritual life with particular value for assessing what might be going on in the wider culture, and the combination of quantitative and qualitative methodologies employed by the team of researchers from Lancaster offers a more nuanced perspective than could be gleaned from a more random statistical analysis.

Some of the detailed understandings offered by this study will be relevant to later chapters in this book, and will be considered in more detail there. But the overall conclusion about the relative strength of New Spirituality vis-à-vis traditional religion (in this case the churches) is worth noting here. It might seem likely that, if the future offers any possibility of the church remaining at the centre of community life, it would happen in a place like Kendal. The reality, however, is quite different, and the results of this study make depressing reading for the Church and its leaders. The fact that, at the time of the research, the figures for church attendance in Kendal were a mirror image of national figures obtained through a different style of research (7.9 per cent of the population) gives credibility to the projections that are offered. On the one hand, the investigation does not provide evidence for the sort of exponential growth in New Spirituality that some have predicted, and suggests that though this increased by more than 300 per cent during the 1990s, that decade represented 'a golden market opportunity' that is unlikely to be repeated in the immediate future.[30] The authors conclude that a realistic estimate of the strength of New Spirituality would see roughly 3 per cent of the population of the UK actively involved in it in one way or another by the middle of the twenty-first century – though they admit that, in view of other cultural factors that are impossible to quantify, this estimate may be 'too cautious'.[31] At the same time, they also conclude that by the year 2030 the number of those regularly involved in the Church will have shrunk to only 3 per cent of the population. That figure, however, is based on the most optimistic reading of the evidence, and they note that a more likely scenario could well be that predicted by Peter Brierley, who has calculated that if the Church's rate of decline continues to increase at the same rate as it did in the 1990s, then Christianity would be all but non-existent by 2016, with only about 0.9 per cent of the population of England attending church.[32] Even accepting the conclusions proposed by Heelas and Woodhead, though, if the figures from their research in Kendal were to be repeated all over the country, then organized Christianity would be virtually extinct in England within little more than twenty years, while the impact of New Spirituality would continue to grow. There are of course various nuances to predictions of this sort, and the authors themselves raise the possibility that New Spirituality might also face some of the same challenges as the churches (e.g. in relation to the age profile of those who are involved, whom they found to be predominantly in the over-45 years age group). Nevertheless, their findings do tend to confirm the general impression that can be gained from less structured analysis of cultural trends, that 'spirituality' is in, and 'religion' is increasingly out as a viable lifestyle choice.

Currents and cross-currents in daily life

As long ago as the mid-1980s, Michel de Certeau, one of the pioneers of what is now known as Cultural Studies, highlighted the importance of listening to what he called the 'absent voice' of ordinary people, and developed an entire methodology that revolves around collecting stories of how people 'make do' and then using such stories to 'provide the decorative container of a *narrativity* for everyday practices'.[33] To describe such a container with precision, one would need to carry out a detailed ethnographic study of the concerns of today's spiritual searchers, which is beyond the scope of this book and the lectures on which it is based. It is nevertheless worth reflecting in a more general way on some of the reasons for the move from 'religion' to 'spirituality' in relation to the experiences of everyday life, before concluding this chapter by identifying some specific intellectual and cultural trends that have contributed to the emergence of New Spirituality at this point in time. Most of these general factors are sufficiently obvious and well attested that they do not need to be justified in detail. But they are worth noting, if only to remind ourselves that most people who adopt beliefs and practices – whether 'spiritual' or 'religious' – do so not for any great ideological reasons, but because of the existential imperative of getting from one day to the next in as meaningful and painless a way as possible.

Life expectancy

An obvious reason for today's increased awareness of spiritual issues is the simple fact that *we are now living for longer*, and – notwithstanding all the financial crises which increasingly bother our politicians as the average age of the population grows older – overall, we are richer than previous generations. Not only do we live for longer, but significant numbers of people (especially of the baby boomer generation) have been able to retire from active employment at a relatively young age. Those who retire at age fifty or fifty-five might easily have more time ahead of them than their entire working life up to that point. It is only to be expected that, faced with the need to make life meaningful without the structure offered by employment, people will have a greater sense of urgency about asking ultimate questions of identity and purpose than previous generations who typically worked until age sixty-five, and then expected to live for no more than a further five or ten years. When a longer life expectancy is combined with more time and money, the spiritual search easily becomes a second vocation.

Freedom and happiness

That is not, of course, the entire picture. For in order to aspire to such a lifestyle in the future, increasing numbers of us are having to work ever longer hours. Such individuals are, to use the jargon, cash rich and time poor – a combination that frequently leads to stress and personal burnout. *We can no longer take it for granted that material prosperity will be naturally associated with happiness*. Moreover, the search for a meaningful life in itself tends to entail disruption and disconnection from those traditional networks of support that enabled previous generations to handle high levels of stress and alienation. Nor is ambition the only factor at work here, for the disruption created by war, poverty and violence is destabilizing populations all over the world, as people move to find places of safety and economic security. In the process, relationships are the one thing that almost invariably suffer, and family fragmentation for one reason or another is an unavoidable consequence. Traditional community networks can sometimes look like fetters that limit an individual's potential by restricting options to a particular place and lifestyle. But at their best, they also provided our forebears with a natural network of support. In a previous generation, those who needed advice on the sort of matters we now describe as 'spiritual' would most often have consulted either an older member of their own immediate family, or a trusted leader of the wider community (typically the parish priest). Today, however, neither of those options would be accessible for most of us: our families are scattered, and for all the reasons mentioned earlier few of us have a living connection to the church, or indeed to other local institutions. This is especially true of Britain, though in the USA Harvard Business School professors Joseph Pine and James Gilmore identify this trend as one of the major business opportunities of the twenty-first century in their own culture, claiming that people are looking for 'experiences to learn and grow, develop and improve, mend and reform . . . [such] transformations turn aspirants into a "new you", with . . . ethical, philosophical, and religious implications . . . We see people seeking spiritual growth outside the bounds of their local, traditional place of worship . . .'[34]

Personal openness

Another contributory factor to the growing interest in 'spirituality' is the fact that *there is generally more openness today in revealing our inner lives*. This is partly driven by the rise of celebrity culture, in which people can evidently become rich and famous by talking about themselves – their weaknesses as well as their strengths, and their aspirations for the future. This is the underlying rationale of reality TV shows such as *Big Brother*, not to mention confessional programmes like *Trisha* or *Jerry Springer* as well as more overtly 'spiritual' programmes such as *Oprah*. If the people who appear on these shows can somehow find themselves by exposing their innermost thoughts, that is a strong incentive for the rest of us to follow their example. Moreover, there is a significant body of psychological evidence to suggest that this kind of thing is good for us, spearheaded by the research of the likes of Carl Gustav Jung (1875–1961), Abraham Maslow (1908–70), Carl Rogers (1902–87), Frederick S. ('Fritz') Perls (1893–1970) and others.[35] All these individuals had their own distinctive spiritual orientations: Jung was so fascinated by ancient Gnosticism that one of the documents from the ancient Nag Hammadi Gnostic library is even named after him,[36] while the others were all instrumental in the emergence of alternative spirituality in California in the 1960s. Moreover, once we start talking to each other about our innermost thoughts, many of us talk about things that more analytical discourse has regarded as taboo, and we realize that a concern for spiritual purpose is nothing like as weird as the prevailing culture had led us to believe. Experiences that might otherwise be dismissed as irrational become harder to discredit when they are part of a personal story – and it is easy to conclude that, if such things have enriched one person's life, then perhaps we should all seek them for ourselves.

Fear

A fourth reason for the increasing concern with spirituality has only come into play following the 9/11 attacks on the USA, and the aftermath that led to the so-called 'war on terrorism'. There were plenty of reasons to be fearful before that, of course, but because the turmoil was mostly restricted to non-western locations, it was not hard for westerners to play down its significance or even overlook it entirely. But we can no longer hide from the reality that *things are in a bigger mess than we thought*. Writing in

2003, Astronomer Royal and Cambridge academic Sir Martin Rees ventured the opinion that,

> I think the odds are no better than fifty-fifty that our present civilization on Earth will survive to the end of the present century . . . What happens here on Earth, in this century, could conceivably make the difference between a near eternity filled with ever more complex and subtle forms of life and one filled with nothing but base matter.[37]

In all times and places, fear has been a powerful catalyst for concentrating attention on the ultimate realities of life, death, purpose, meaning, and identity.[38]

Diversity

In parallel with this, *we know more of the world than any previous generation*, and we know it differently. For our Western forebears, the world was 'out there' in other countries and other cultures. To encounter 'the other', Western people had to travel, which meant that only a tiny number actually did. But today, the world is increasingly also 'in here', in all its fascinating and threatening diversity. Though most cities still have a long way to go before they catch up with Los Angeles, to one degree or another all our communities are fast becoming microcosms of the global reality. As part of that, not only are Western people aware of the existence of a vast array of possible different world views, but they are also curious to know more about them. When natural curiosity is combined with the growth of consumerism, which offers an infinite number of choices in everything from coffee to clothing, the emergence of the spiritual supermarket becomes a natural development, and once established it is inevitable that the range of goods on offer there will also expand to fill the space available.

Spiritual search

As it happens, in roughly the same time frame (the second half of the twentieth century) the decline of the Christian Church as a credible locus for meaningful spirituality meant that the cloth out of which Western values and ultimate meanings were historically woven was itself looking increasingly threadbare. When a culture and its spiritual guides simultaneously experience the kind of failure of nerve that we are witnessing today, a spiritual vacuum is the inevitable result. In such circumstances, people do not believe in nothing: they look for fresh ways to express their search for meaning, and embrace those spiritual pathways that appear to be most adequately contextualized in the realities of their own lives. Or, to continue the previous metaphor, they reweave the cloth using whatever threads – both old and new – come to hand. In such a circumstance, it is no surprise to find novelist Douglas Coupland writing a book with the title *Life after God* and reminding his readers that 'you are the first generation raised without religion'. But we know that things are infinitely more complex than that when he continues by posing the following questions:

> 'What happens if we are raised without religion or beliefs? As we grow older, the beauty and disenchantments of the world temper our souls. We are all living creatures with strong religious impulses, yet where do these impulses flow in a world of malls and TV, Kraft dinner and jets?'[39]

Even the most attentive reader is likely to be surprised when, some 350 pages later, Coupland makes his final confession:

> Now – here is my secret:
> I tell it to you with an openness of heart that I doubt I shall ever achieve again, so I pray that you are in a quiet room as you hear these words. My secret is that I need God – that I am sick and can no longer make it alone. I need God to help me give, because I no longer seem to be capable of giving; to help me be kind, as I no longer seem capable of kindness; to help me love, as I seem beyond being able to love.[40]

There is no apology here for speaking of God – 'God' is not even in quotes – but equally, there is no hint that God is likely to be found in organizations or institutions. This is spirituality without religion, a search for God that begins with personal experience and reaches out from there to look for possible answers, rather than starting with the answers and attempting to bring human experience into line with them. This fact alone should make it easy for Christians to connect with today's spiritual search. Far from being some post-modern subversion of faith, it seems to me that this sort of enquiry is a natural consequence of the biblical affirmation that people are 'made in God's image' (Genesis 1:27-8). It is also the underlying pattern of conversion that is taken for granted throughout the New Testament, and reaffirmed by many recent theological methodologies, not the least of which is to be located in my own discipline of 'practical theology'.[41] I have already jumped ahead of the argument with that observation, but it is sufficiently important to be worth noting here even though we will not return to it in any depth until the final chapter. In the meantime, we need to dig a bit deeper beneath the surface of Western culture to unearth some of the scientific and philosophical trends that have brought us to this place.

Historical perspectives

Post-modern people have mixed feelings about history. On the one hand, the effort to deconstruct what previous generations thought they knew about the past has created a suspicious and cynically destructive attitude to those who went before us. On the other hand, whether we like it or not, we cannot escape the influence of our own personal and national histories. Nor can we rewrite the past – though we can learn from it and, more often than we think, it is possible to redeem it. The well-known Chinese proverb still contains more than a grain of truth with its reminder that 'whoever does not know the village they have come from will never find the village they are looking for'. We are certainly looking for a new village today, but it is the past that will help to explain why Douglas Coupland could claim without fear of contradiction that we are indeed 'the first generation raised without religion' – and in the process of understanding that, we may be led to a deeper understanding of what it is that we are looking for, and a tentative definition of what we mean when we now speak of spirituality.

This is neither the time nor the place to engage in an exhaustive review of the cultural trends that have contributed to the development of Western culture. But there are some fundamental factors that have been decisive in determining our perception of who we are, where we have come from, and what we are about – those major questions that Walter Truett Anderson calls 'the Big Three: cosmology, identity, and epistemology; how you think about the universe, who you think you are, and what you believe about belief'.[42]

It has become fashionable in recent years – especially among Christians – to blame 'the Enlightenment' for all the woes of a post-modern world. But 'the Enlightenment' and 'post-modernity' are both problematic categories. I am not using these words with any technical or narrowly defined meaning here, but rather as a rough and ready way of referring to two widely attested realities. 'The Enlightenment' is a shorthand way of referring to the world view that has prevailed in the West for roughly the past 500 years, while 'post-modernity' will serve as a way of describing the chaos into which things have descended once that world view began to be questioned and rejected. It will be the job of future generations to decide whether post-modernity turns out to be anything more substantial than that, though on the basis of all the available evidence right now it strikes me as unlikely that 'post-modernity' represents any sort of coherent world view. Use of the term gives the appearance of rationality to discussions about contemporary culture, which no doubt explains why it has become so popular. But to paraphrase Marx's famous dictum, 'post-modernity' is the opiate of the intelligentsia, a make-believe expression that encourages academics to think they understand what is going on in the world – and behind that is the thought that if we are able to name it correctly, we will also be able to control it. This is just fantasy and wishful thinking: Western civilization is in a bigger mess than most of us care to admit. It may be in a phase of final meltdown. What happens next is certainly not within the power of either academics or politicians – or multinational corporations – to determine.

We are on safer ground in trying to grasp what the Enlightenment was about, because we were not a part of it and can now stand back and see a bigger picture. The one thing we can say with certainty is that – like the paradigm shift that is going on today – the Enlightenment was not a single event, entity or idea, but consisted of many different strands that gradually combined over a period of two or three centuries so as to effect a massive change of world view among European people. The map of the world was – from a European perspective – quite literally redrawn, as previously unknown lands were not only explored but annexed to European kingdoms. The elevation of human reason to a position as final arbiter of all human wisdom opened up new conceptual horizons in everything from navigation to surgery and theological knowledge, and the rise of technology and industrialization created new ways of doing things that led to the reshaping of the family as paid work moved from the home to the factory, and the first generation of consumers was born. One of the most influential strands of thinking that fed into all this came from the Church, more specifically from the Protestant Reformation with its emphasis on the importance of each individual having a direct and unmediated relationship with God. Paradoxically, when this insistence was translated into the political and intellectual arena, it not only had the effect of marginalizing the Church as a meaningful spiritual community, but also created the conditions out of which faith itself could be banished from public life and redefined as a private and personal matter for individuals, for whom the ultimate expression of personhood would now be the Cartesian ideal of the autonomous rational individual endued with the ability to transform themselves and intentionally reinvent human culture.

It is not difficult to trace a linear development from that through to the present situation in which religion is replaced by spirituality, and in which the spiritual quest is largely a search for privatized and internalized meaning, at the same time as we all yearn for a sense of meaningful community where we can not only be accepted but also find our true destiny and ultimate identity. Over the centuries, many factors have contributed to this shift, and it is probably the case that the combination of them all has been more influential than any of them might have been separately. But some developments have undoubtedly played a more obviously important role in the emergence of today's spiritual search, and three in particular strike me as having played an especially crucial role: the theory of evolution in the nineteenth century, the emergence of psychotherapy in the mid years of the twentieth century, and the growth of consumerism, globalization, and McDonaldization in the 1980s and 1990s.

Charles Darwin and the theory of evolution

Charles Darwin (1809–82) is best known for his epic contribution to the understanding of the nature of life itself. But his scientific work on biology also had hidden implications for the evolution of society, which I believe has contributed to the emergence of New Spirituality in our own generation. The ideas that Darwin promoted did not come out of nowhere, but like all great thinkers he just happened to be in the right place at the right time. The environment in which he operated was one in which his theories could take root quite easily. The Britain of his day already had a strong philosophical commitment to the idea that progress in all things was inevitable, a conviction that was visibly embodied in political confidence and military accomplishment as the empire was expanded over much of the earth's surface, bringing with it the expectation that it would only be a matter of time before the unenlightened peoples of the non-western world would be redeemed from their savagery and 'civilized' by their exposure to the scientific wisdom of the age, along with a certain sort of Christian belief.[43] In a world where it seemed that everything was changing after centuries of stagnation, as superstitious darkness gave way to the illumination of Western ideas, it was natural to wonder if the same sort of development might also extend – over a much longer timescale – to include the very fabric of life itself. The groundwork had already been laid for this with the publication of Charles Lyell's *Principles of Geology* in which he challenged the accepted view that the continents had been created in a single moment of time, and suggested instead that they had come about through natural geological events that took place over the course of millions of years.[44]

When Darwin applied the same logic to human life, it challenged not only the received wisdom among biologists, but also had far-reaching implications for many other aspects of social organization. The resistance of church leaders to Darwinian theory has been well documented, though that was not actually the point at which his ideas made their greatest impact in terms of cultural change. The truth is that not all Christians opposed his ideas, nor did all scientists accept them. Nor for that matter did Darwin himself see any necessary contradiction between his scientific observations and his own Christian faith – about which he was well enough informed, for after studying medicine in Edinburgh he went on to Cambridge to study theology with a view to becoming a priest in the Church of England. In his classic work *The Origin of Species*, published in 1859, he explicitly affirmed a supernaturalist view of the origins of life, expressed in a hymn-like way in the final sentence of the book as he concluded that 'There is grandeur in this view of life, with its several powers, having been originally breathed [by the Creator] into a few forms or into one . . .'[45]

Though the theological implications of Darwin's ideas are still debated in some circles, it is the cultural implications of his theory that have arguably had the most far-reaching impact, for he challenged our understanding of who we think we really are. In terms of scientific thinking, Darwin laid to rest once and for all the Cartesian-Newtonian consensus of his day, which had proceeded on the assumption that humans were both intrinsically different from other life forms, and also vastly superior to animals and plants. Within that, of course, it was also widely held that there was a kind of rising scale of what it meant to be fully human, with white Western males at the pinnacle of that hierarchy, and other types of people placed in a descending order of humanness until, at the bottom of the pile, were the original inhabitants of Australia, who were not regarded as biologically human until the early years of the twentieth century, and had to wait even longer for their psychological and spiritual worth to be affirmed. It took some time for all the implications of Darwin's discoveries to be fully appreciated, but the consequences were inescapable: if people were biologically connected to the whole of creation, rather than separate from it, then humans could no longer think of their own existence as being detached from the rest of the cosmos. That realization had within it the potential for undermining the very foundations of science itself, for it would be a contradiction in terms to think of any individual operating as a detached observer, looking in from the outside at natural phenomena – and that in turn meant that the autonomous rational individual so beloved of Descartes was nothing more than a figment of his imagination.

If Darwin challenged the accepted understanding of who we are in relation to the natural world, his ideas had even more profound implications for the future of the British class system, and ultimately for the ways in which decisions are made and how human wisdom is evaluated. The class system of his day was a social mirror image of the biological concept of a 'great chain of being', which envisaged different species operating within a hierarchical system that had been established for all time in accordance with the will of God. Even after Darwin's time, this view was perpetuated in many hymns ('The rich man in his castle, the poor man at his gate . . .'), and continued to be influential in British culture. Some would argue that it still is. But even before Darwin it had already been challenged in other places, most notably at the time of the French Revolution, and again in the post-civil war period of American history. The American Declaration of Independence (1776) declared it to be a 'self-evident truth' we are all 'endowed by the Creator with certain unalienable rights', and the first to be listed was the right to 'life, liberty and the pursuit of happiness' – a slogan which rather neatly correlates with some fundamental concerns in the New Spirituality.

We have already noted how this period of American history coincided with the rise of many novel spiritual movements, and the emergence of a new egalitarian society no doubt provided a catalyst for this. Similar trends can be traced in France at the time of the Revolution there, where a new social model coincided with the development of a fresh interest in spirituality, graphically portrayed in Charles Dickens's description of aristocratic city life:

> The leprosy of unreality disfigured every human creature in attendance upon Monseigneur. In the outermost room were half a dozen exceptional people who had had, for a few years, some vague misgiving in them that things in general were going rather wrong. As a promising way of setting them right, half of the half-dozen had become members of a

> fantastic sect of Convulsionists, and were even then considering within themselves whether they should foam, rage, roar, and turn cataleptic on the spot – thereby setting up a highly intelligible finger-post to the Future, for Monseigneur's guidance. Besides these Dervishes, were other three who had rushed into another sect, which mended matters with a jargon about 'the Centre of Truth': holding that Man had got out of the Centre of Truth . . . but had not got out of the Circumference, and that he was to be kept from flying out of the Circumference, and was even to be shoved back into the Centre, by fasting and seeing of spirits. Among these, accordingly, much discoursing with spirits went on . . .[46]

It was in France at the same period that the Tarot (which had originated as southern European playing cards in the fourteenth century) was reinvented as a way of connecting with spiritual realities, as aristocratic families sought to maintain their élite status by their involvement in esoteric practices, encouraged by their Protestant pastors, most notably Antoine Court de Gebelin. According to Carl Raschke, this is invariably the context in which new forms of spiritual fascination have surfaced over the centuries:

> A social élite gradually surrenders its leadership functions and devotes its energies to letters and learning . . . their painful isolation from the culture of the masses leading to a self-enforced pariah mentality, expressed in both their contempt for legitimate authority and their creation of a closed symbolic universe which only those with the proper credentials can penetrate . . . the safekeeping of magical lore reflects a vicarious exercise of power which in reality has slipped away from them.[47]

What is less well attested, but no less significant, is the close correlation between Darwin's ideas and the beliefs espoused by some of the new spiritual movements of the nineteenth and early twentieth centuries. The messages that Joseph Smith, founder of Mormonism, received from angelic beings provide a remarkable theological parallel with the theory of evolution, most strikingly through the doctrine of 'eternal progression' in which it is proposed that the Heavenly Father began as a human who, with his wife, 'progressed' to become divine – something that ultimately was claimed to be within the evolutionary possibility of all of us. Indeed, Smith propounded this evolutionary principle as a basic law of the universe, guaranteeing that 'gods, angels, and men are all of one species, one race, one great family' and that people existed as spirits before evolving into embodied beings, and would ultimately evolve even further to take over other planets.[48] Within a British context, it is possible to trace a similar trend towards evolutionary thinking in the emergence of dispensational theology among the Plymouth Brethren, promoted by John Nelson Darby (1800–82) and later popularized especially through the *Scofield Reference Bible*.[49] This regarded the whole of human history as being divided into different epochs, or dispensations, with more of God's ultimate purposes being revealed in each one until eventually the world as we know it would end, with the establishment of new heavens and a new earth. Though some Brethren leaders – most famously, Philip Gosse[50] – adopted a publicly hostile stance with regard to biological evolution, it is hard to avoid the conclusion that the underlying rationale of the theological system they created was just one variation of a fundamentally evolutionary way of understanding the world and its people.

Existentialism, psychoanalysis and new science

It was inevitable that the new understanding of the biological relationship between people and the natural world should have an impact on other, more intimate, aspects of human self-understanding. Nineteenth-century thinkers were able to build on the work of Darwin, and embrace a vision of a future filled with hope and unstoppable progress. But as early as the 1930s, the brutal realities of life in Europe not only made that seem implausible, but the work of existential thinkers was suggesting that we would only find freedom and purpose in life not by speculating about where we have come from, but by facing the most ultimate fact of all about ourselves, namely that we exist in the here and now. There is no consensus as to whether this emphasis was sufficiently cogent to qualify as a movement in any organized sense, but the focus on the human subject and his or her self-understanding as the key to the good life helped to create an intellectual seedbed in which one of the major components of New Spirituality would be able to take root and flourish. Existentialism in itself presupposed no particular religious or political frame of reference, and its leading exponents included Nietzsche (an atheist), Søren Kierkegaard (a Christian), Jean-Paul Sartre (a left-winger) and Martin Heidegger (a right-winger). But the Jewish thinker Martin Buber made a significant contribution to what was to follow with his insistence that, like everything else, the full meaning of 'God' was to be found in the present moment, rather than through abstract historical or theoretical discourse. Drawing on the insights of Hasidism, he explored what it might mean if the whole of life was to be sacralized, and proposed that 'God' was present in interpersonal relationships as people were open to others for themselves (the 'I-Thou' relationship) rather than judging others on the basis of external knowledge about them (the 'I-It' relationship). One of the reasons why more rationally orientated thinkers have never been able to decide if existentialism was a real philosophical system is because of its emphasis on the encounter of the individual with his or her most intimate self. But the same experiential base that created problems for more traditional philosophers was the very thing that commended it to the world of psychotherapy which, though having a very different starting point, centred around a potentially transformational existential encounter between therapist and client.

Existentialism disappeared without trace in the years immediately following the Second World War, but provided a bridge between Darwinism and some of the most powerful cultural influences of the 1960s' revolution, especially in its Californian version (which, because of its scholarly base, not to mention the power of the Hollywood media, became the definitive intellectual expression of the new emerging world view). When combined with the ideas of psychologists like Rollo May, Carl Rogers and Abraham Maslow, the 'existential moment' spoken of more abstractly by European thinkers took flesh in a form that made it accessible to everyone, and became the key to meaningful self-understanding. In the early part of the twentieth century, psychology had been dominated by the behaviourists, on the one hand, and Sigmund Freud on the other. The behavioural approach inevitably downplayed the experience of the self by suggesting that we are essentially animals conditioned to respond in predictable ways to environmental impulses, while Freud famously saw people as neurotics driven by irrational – and unconscious – desires. Neither of these opinions fitted well with the self-understanding of the 1960s, in which a new-found freedom enabled the boundaries of human consciousness to be pushed to new and higher limits. Those who experimented with mind-bending drugs that opened up new levels of consciousness just *knew* that human potential was far greater than anyone had previously imagined to be possible.[51] And they knew it because of their experiences: human beings, when released from all inhibitions, could quite literally become masters of the universe. Alan Watts, an English academic and some-time Episcopalian priest, was just such an experimenter, and in the title of one of his books he mentions 'the Taboo against knowing who you are'[52] – a taboo that had been imposed by cultural control and reinforced by science, and which he and others like him were determined to break.

In the process of seeking to do this, it was possible to build on the work of earlier psychologists such as William James and Carl Gustav Jung, both of whom were regarded as mavericks because not only were they interested in researching 'religious experience', but they also took it seriously as a key to human happiness. But none of the key players in the early development of psychotherapy held religious beliefs in more than a perfunctory way. In the words of Alan Watts, 'We do not need a new religion or a new bible. We need a new experience . . .'[53] Though he was himself deeply interested in Buddhism, he regarded it as neither a belief system nor a distinctive world view, but as a form of personal therapy – and Buddhism thus redefined just happened to confirm the practices of therapists such as May and Rogers, who had insisted all along that following rules and dogma was not the way to a happy life.[54] Out of the many meetings held at the Esalen Institute and informed by the empirical research carried out by Maslow among workers in the industrial cities of the

Midwest, there emerged the idea that the sort of experiences that William James had previously classified as 'religious' were actually human experiences, and rather than being spoken of as encounters with 'God' they would be better understood as 'self-actualization'. In the process of this redefinition, the circumstances were created in which spirituality could be separated from religion. Somewhat paradoxically, it is only more recently that practical psychotherapy has begun to take spirituality seriously and regard it in a positive light.[55]

Running parallel with this was another revolution of thought that would also feed into the emergence of New Spirituality, this time coming out of the world of 'hard' physical science rather than the 'softer' insights of human science. Darwin challenged the Cartesian view that had seen a clear separation between humans and nature, but it was Albert Einstein's theory of relativity that provided the theoretical base from which the consequences of that could be fully explored. For Californian scientists, the cultural upheaval that began in the 1960s provided the catalyst for reflecting on the spiritual significance of the interconnectedness of humankind with the natural world. One of the leading lights in this exploration was Fritjof Capra, physics professor at the University of California in Berkeley. The title of one of his earliest books, *The Tao of Physics*, indicates the direction of his thinking, as he sought to connect sub-atomic physics with ancient mysticism.[56] In a later book, he makes the spiritual connection quite explicit: 'The new concepts in physics have brought about a profound change in our world view; from the mechanistic conception of Descartes and Newton to a holistic or ecological view, a view which I have found to be similar to the views of mystics of all ages and traditions.'[57] He was not the only scientist to think in this way. Niels Bohr was another one who viewed his research in a spiritual light, claiming that he was engaged with the very same 'epistemological problems with which already thinkers like the Buddha and Lao Tzu have been confronted, when trying to harmonize our position as spectators and actors in the great drama of existence'.[58]

This heady mixture of psychological and scientific research, combined with experimental lifestyles and consciousness-expanding experiences, helped to create a mindset that regarded human potential as limitless and saw the future as a time of unparalleled prosperity and harmony, if only humankind would break away from all that held it back (which, of course, included religion) and take control of its own evolutionary future. Marilyn Ferguson's epic book *The Aquarian Conspiracy* is brimming with such optimism:

> The paradigm of the Aquarian conspiracy sees humankind embedded in nature. It promotes the autonomous individual in a decentralized society. It sees us as stewards of our resources, inner and outer. It says that we are not victims, not pawns, not limited by conditions and conditioning.[59]

Like those others already mentioned, Ferguson was a professor (psychology). But such expectations were not limited to academics. When *New Age Journal* conducted a survey in 1987 inviting readers to share their hopes for the coming new age, one individual described it as 'ultimately a vision of a world transformed, a heaven on earth, a society in which the problems of today are overcome and a new existence emerges', while another wrote of 'moving into an era that emphasizes self-discovery, spiritual growth, and enlightenment'.[60] Much has changed in the intervening years, but many of today's spiritual searchers still share a similar dream.

Consumerism, globalization, McDonaldization

Marilyn Ferguson's *Aquarian Conspiracy* was published in the USA in 1980. In November of that year, Ronald Reagan was elected fortieth American president, and just a year before that Margaret Thatcher had become prime minister of the United Kingdom. Their dominance of the Western world throughout the 1980s was another formative influence that helped create the atmosphere in which the concerns that we now identify as New Spirituality could not only emerge and flourish, but also be transformed into a big business. Trying to second-guess what is in the minds of politicians will always be just that – guesswork. But there are several points at which the global capitalism unleashed by the Reagan-Thatcher years connects with implicit values that can be traced back to the 1960s' cultural revolution.

One thing of which there can be no doubt is the emphasis that Margaret Thatcher in particular placed on the potential of the individual. She famously declared that she did not believe there was any such thing as society, only individuals and families. This was clearly not an isolated unguarded statement, for the importance of individuals taking responsibility for themselves, and creating their own future, was reinforced by her own government ministers and enshrined in their policies. Thatcher and Reagan both publicly projected a conservative and traditional religious image, but their understanding of personal accountability was often indistinguishable from some of the most extreme advocates of the power of human potential. This statement from *The Emerging New Age* by sociology professor J.L. Simmons exactly mirrors the political ideology of the day:

> We create the realities we experience, consciously or unknowingly. The universe ultimately gives us what we ask for . . . Since we construct our own lives, it is false and misleading to blame others for what we are experiencing . . . The buck stops with us. And change is in our own hands.[61]

The amoral nature of such ideas, with the clear implication that, if the rich are responsible for making themselves rich, then the poor must also be responsible for their poverty, set the tone for much that has happened in Western society in the last twenty years. Of course, the hope was that by creating a global market, everyone would have the opportunity to become rich. Capitalism could envisage no limit on human capacity – a notion that dovetailed rather neatly with ideas from the human potential movement which provided another stream of ideas feeding into the New Spirituality. Moreover, the rise of global capitalism can be portrayed as an example of how all things are indeed interconnected, thereby fulfilling one of the core aspirational values of the alternative spiritualities and lifestyles of the 1960s. In view of the calls for a 'back to nature' lifestyle often voiced by New Spirituality activists – and occasionally expressed as opposition to the operations of multinational corporations – this connection may come as a surprise, but it is nonetheless inescapable. When consumerism and New Spirituality meet, the outcome is

> a virtually unprecedented level of spiritual independence and commercialism together. People get fragments of Tibet or Chaldea in an enlightenment emporium and practice it on their own at home, apart from any living priest or temple, with a confidence both wonderful and appalling, with an attitude less of credence than of, Let's check it out, and I'll take from it what I can use.[62]

The notion of shopping as therapy takes on a whole new meaning when this is the stuff that people are buying!

This connection has recently been subjected to critical scrutiny by Jeremy Carrette and Richard King, who argue that the rise of New Spirituality is driven – and may even have been created – by the expansion of global capitalism. Put simply, they propose that consumerism creates a particular form of human exploitation which contributes to the general feeling of malaise and meaninglessness that characterizes the experience of so many people today, and the marketing of spirituality is a method of making money out of the *angst* that this way of being has created in the first place. In documenting this 'corporate takeover of all human knowledge and life',[63] Carrette and King's cynicism knows no limits: New Spirituality is 'cultural prozac . . . [which] exacerbates the problems of meaning associated with materialism and individualism in the very desire for some kind of escape from the world. Such capitalist spiritualities thereby end up reinforcing the very problems that many of its advocates seek to overcome'. Moreover, 'In the very act of freeing the mind from the dogma of religion, consumers now entered the thought-control of individualism.'[64] In the process, the riches of various traditional religious traditions are ransacked in such a way that '. . . "spirituality" has . . . become the brand name for the act of selling off the assets of "old time" religion [which still] . . . have "cachet value" for a society of isolated individuals, hungry for packaged meaning.'[65]

There is plenty of evidence for the kind of commercialization of spirituality which Carrette and King describe, but that is not the whole picture. As long ago as 1989, the self-styled 'Jewitch' Starhawk was complaining about people who are starved of spiritual resources in their own culture and who 'unwittingly become spiritual strip miners damaging other cultures in superficial attempts to uncover their mystical treasures'.[66] A decade later, Islamic scholar Ziauddin Sardar highlighted the imperialistic attitudes implicit in the selective adoption of traditional religious ideas when he observed that, 'when western thought reaches a dead end, it unreservedly turns towards [other cultures] to appropriate and devour [their] thought and continue on its irrational and grotesquely skewed goal . . . [which turns out to be] simply a new wave of domination riding on the crest of colonialism and modernity.'[67] The fact is that the opportunity for the commercial exploitation of the contemporary search for meaning is itself a natural spin-off of the emergence of a so-called 'post-modern' mindset. I have already expressed my own doubts as to the coherence of the notion that 'post-modernity' represents any sort of consistent world view, but there can be no doubt that certain strands of philosophical thinking have helped to create the context in which this 'wholesale commodification of religion'[68] could thrive. On the one hand, though the meaningfulness of metanarratives has been questioned, the very existence of New Spirituality is evidence that the personal search for some big story that might be worth giving one's life for has not diminished but has actually intensified. On the other the hermeneutic of suspicion, which has placed a question mark against the motives of all previous generations of religious leaders, has so devalued the spiritual wisdom of the past that we are indeed cast adrift on a sea of consumer choice as the only possible way forward.

The deconstruction of religion could easily form the subject of an entire chapter, if not another book. For those not familiar with the notion of 'deconstruction', it might be defined somewhat simply as looking at the reverse side of history – recognizing that the narratives we inherit have come from those who won, and seeking to view the past from different perspectives. Looked at in this way, the story of Christian history is frequently regarded as something dark and regressive, if not actually demonic. It is not difficult to identify how various power struggles have affected the development of Christianity. The adoption of Christianity as the official faith of the Roman empire by Constantine in 312 raises the question of whether he was converted or the original faith was corrupted, while similar issues arise in connection with the various arguments over the formulation of the creeds in subsequent centuries and, in Britain, the decisions of the Synod of Whitby (663–4) at which the Roman version of faith succeeded in banishing an originally Celtic form of Christian belief. Following that, things merely went from bad to worse with the emergence of the Holy Roman Empire and Christendom, and the imposition of this world view on other peoples, first through the Crusades and then through colonialism. If we throw into the mixture the way that later missionary movements aided the expansion of the British empire, accompanied by the suppression of traditional world views in favour of Enlightenment ideas of reason and progress – and the mess this has created for so many of the world's people – it is not difficult to see why Christians are having a hard time. When all this is combined with the institutionalized patriarchy of many churches, and the support of Christian nations for territorial expansion even today, it is easy to see the attraction of what Carrette and King call 'a Genetically Modified Religion'[69] that will take the best of the tradition and jettison the rest. Of course, many aspects of that summary of a deconstructed Christian history can be questioned, but enough of it is grounded in fact to suggest that, instead of detailed point-scoring, those Christians who wish to make any contribution to the spiritual search of our day will need to engage with all this at a much deeper level than before.

Carrette and King have done a good job of drawing attention to the commercialization of spirituality and its consequences not only for religion but for any meaningful future for Western civilization. But their argument ultimately lacks a durable foundation because of their uncritical acceptance of what (despite their claims to the contrary) is actually a different metanarrative, namely the notion that *'There is no essence or definitive meaning to terms like spirituality or religion.'*[70] If that is the case, then their plea for a faith that will offer a meaningful alternative to 'a form of thought-control that supports the ideology of late capitalism'[71] is likely to fall on deaf ears. For it is only in the specificity of religious traditions that one finds a challenge to the status quo. In particular, New Spirituality – whether or not it is viewed as a consumer product – tends to have little to say about suffering and injustice. The challenge for the Church, though, is that increasing numbers of people find that what it offers has also been reduced to a McDonaldized product and a growing body of people find themselves disenchanted with the churches, and not infrequently their disillusionment is in direct proportion to their concern for maintaining core Christian values. Alan Jamieson is only the most recent researcher to have produced empirical evidence showing that people of all ages (including some lifelong church leaders) are finding themselves forced to leave the Church in order to follow Christ more faithfully.[72]

In the meantime, others are engaged on a serious personal search for spiritual tools that will enable them to overcome past hurts, realize future hopes, and empower them to live effectively by awakening a spiritual connection. They are doing this by sampling from a remarkably diverse range of spiritual tools or disciplines that include things as simple as good food and friendship, as well as more exotic high energy experiences. How all these things might be regarded as 'spiritual' is the subject of our next chapter.

2 Spirituality in Everyday Life

Having looked briefly at some of the reasons – historical, cultural and religious – for the rising tide of interest in what Western culture now unashamedly calls 'the spiritual', we need to try and come up with some sort of definition of what it is that counts as being spiritual these days. In one sense, I have already given an answer to that question: spirituality is the opposite of what religion is now perceived to be. In particular, where religion is regarded as controlling, prescriptive, narrow-minded, and ultimately damaging, spirituality is life-giving, nurturing, and personally empowering. A fair number of writers regard this as a problem, and dismiss the current interest in spirituality as shallow and meaningless, and perhaps even more damaging than religion is supposed to be. Theology professor Stephen Pattison describes it disparagingly as 'bespoke metaphysical marshmallow that is non-specific, unlocated, thin, uncritical, dull and un-nutritious',[1] while Carrette and King complain that '"spirituality" has . . . become the brand name for the act of selling off the assets of "old time" religion . . . for a society of isolated individuals hungry for packaged meaning'.[2] From a purely phenomenological angle, it is not difficult to see why the very slipperiness of the term should provoke such negative comments. My primary concern here, however, is not phenomenological but missiological. I want to understand not only what it is that motivates us to search for spiritual meaning in life, but also how that might connect with what it means to be Christian in the twenty-first century. In order to do that, we will need to take seriously the starting points of ordinary folk, and that will not happen if we regard those starting points as inadequate or devoid of meaning. Writing of life in the corporate workplace, Donald W. McCormick argues that many managers find that 'integrating spirituality and work brings profound meaning to their jobs'.[3] If that is the case, then from a

Christian perspective we owe it to such people to listen to what they are saying, and how they are saying it, rather than dismissing their discourse as infantile or intellectually substandard.

That does not mean there are no questions to be raised about the way terminology relating to the spiritual is being used today. But it does mean that I am more inclined to agree with Rodney Clapp's astute observation that 'against conventional grammar, *spirituality* appears to be a noun decisively determined by its adjective'.[4] Whether we like it or not, therefore, in terms of the mission of the Church we need to begin from the recognition that 'spirituality' is being used in many different ways today, and understand it in that frame of reference rather than complaining about the inadequacy of other people's definitions.

I want to propose here that the use of the terms 'spiritual' and 'spirituality' is neither as random nor as shallow as it can be made out to be. It seems to me that there is a continuous thread that connects all the multifarious ways in which we are today searching for spiritual meaning in life. For those who are familiar with it, a useful conceptual framework within which to understand how apparently disparate elements can all belong on the same spectrum of belief and lifestyle would be Wittgenstein's notion of 'family resemblances',[5] while those more familiar with social science perspectives might find the notion of a 'metanetwork', or network of networks,[6] or a SPIN (segmented polycentric integrated network) to be more helpful.[7] It is a bit like the traditional Indian story of a group of blind beggars who tried to describe an elephant. One, starting from the animal's legs, described it as a tree; another, grasping its trunk, assumed it must be a hose; while the third, taking hold of its tail, insisted that an elephant was like a rope. They were all correct, of course, but none of them had the complete picture. We face the same challenge (and the same chance of achieving total accuracy) in attempting to understand the complex entity that is New Spirituality. Using a different metaphor, Donal Dorr describes today's spiritual search as 'a cake into which we have to put a wide variety of ingredients',[8] and in this chapter I want to consider the nature of some of these ingredients. In order to do this, we will first of all consider three different – though typical and representative – approaches to the application of spiritual principles in daily life, on the basis of which I wish to propose a broadly based model within which to unpack contemporary notions of 'spirituality'. In the effort to identify a common thread holding these somewhat disparate uses of the term together, we will then venture into the experimental territory of the emerging discipline of neurotheology. In conclusion there will be some consideration of the relationship between experience and story and the importance of a meaningful metanarrative that will place our connections with the transcendent into a bigger framework than our own individual life experiences, prejudices, and preconceptions. This will then set the scene for later chapters in which we will explore ways in which the Christian story can relate to the many spiritual stories being told in the wider culture, and ask how Christians can with integrity invite others to join them on the journey which is the obedient discipleship of following Jesus Christ.

Spirituality and the business of life

Though I do not share Carrette and King's opinion that we have become interested in being spiritual only because commercial organizations now want to sell us 'spiritual' goodies, it is nevertheless the case that the dominance of globalized capitalism has had an impact on people's lives in such a way that they have been driven to ask big questions about meaning and purpose that would never have occurred in the same way to previous generations. It should therefore surprise no one that the corporate workplace is one of the places where concern to find spiritual solutions to life's problems has emerged as a major training opportunity. As far back as the 1980s, many of the most high-profile experiments in spiritual awareness were to be located within this matrix, some of them controversial and evoking strong feelings among an often traditional workforce. While the highly rationalized world in which multinationals do their business might at first seem like the last place to discover a self-conscious search for spiritual solutions, there is actually a direct connection between the two. For the expansion of the global market, and the consequent pressures experienced by those who work within it, meant that this was the one area of life in which the inadequacy of traditional ways of doing things showed up sooner rather than later. The global economy itself is quite different from older forms of economic activity. The empires of the past might well have created an almost worldwide market for their own products, but the type of globalization that began to emerge in the 1980s was different. It was not merely about the creation of a single market for the products of one nation state, but turned out to be a complex network of networks linked to one another in ways that almost seem to have a life of their own. Moreover, this interactive, interdependent way of relating had many similarities with the emerging scientific consensus about the interrelationship of all things ('the web of life' of which Fritjof Capra and others wrote), and which had already been favourably linked to the insights of mystical spiritual traditions by the leaders of the counterculture in the 1960s. New ways of doing business seemed as if they demanded a new type of world view because the old ways would, quite simply, no longer work. Given the context of global capitalism in which these new ways came to birth, it was inevitable that commercial values would take precedence over human values in the workplace, and the damaging effects of this are now felt throughout the world of work, including what previously would have been regarded as person-centred occupations such as healthcare, education and, increasingly, the Church. Wherever we look, stress is a major problem. In commercial organizations, CEOs are pressurized by shareholders to maximize profits, so they in turn lean on middle managers to increase productivity, and the only way they can reach their targets is by exerting pressure on the workers whom they manage – who, in one of the biggest ironies of the entire scenario, are often themselves shareholders, having been lured to become so by the promise of big profits (most of which never materialize). Nor is this situation unique to the world of big business. Public service bodies such as schools and universities, not to mention healthcare providers, all operate on this model. The outcome is that individuals find themselves personally stressed, but even more worrying in some respects is the way that the resultant competitiveness undermines collaboration in the workforce, and human values like trust and integrity go out of the window. In this environment, it is hardly surprising that hard-pressed individuals will turn to almost anything that appears to offer a way of surviving, even if its effects may be transient. Increasing numbers of people struggle just to make it through from one day to the next.[9]

It was not, however, management consultants who first made the connection between personal beliefs and ways of doing business, but academics who were seeking to understand the wider impact of cultural change on the workplace. One of the most influential of such writers was Russell Ackoff. At one level, his book *Creating the Corporate Future,* published in 1981, said nothing new, and merely applied to the business world insights taken from the work of biologist Ludwig von Bertalanffy, who had promoted a science of context called 'perspectivism', which laid the foundations for what subsequently came to be known as General Systems Theory.[10] Ackoff compared the 'Machine Age' (the old outmoded ways of doing things) with the newly birthed 'Systems Age', which proposed that nothing can fully be understood in isolation, but will only make sense within its total context, or 'system'. Each component in any system therefore interacts with all the other components in such a way that it is both impossible and pointless to try and separate them. James Lovelock had already made a similar argument with regard to the physical environment, and Ackoff and others like him simply extended it into other areas of human interaction and experience.[11]

The influence of 'machine age' thinking is not hard to discern. Many inherited institutions – political, religious, industrial, educational – are bureaucratic and impersonal, operating within rigid mechanistic frameworks that at best lead to fragmentation and conformity, and at worst actually deny the humanity of those who are enmeshed in them. Following the lead given by Einstein, modern science first began to recognize the inadequacy of this understanding a hundred years ago, but it took most of the twentieth century for the consequences of such questioning to be fully understood. Today it is taken for granted that we can no longer continue to do things in the old ways – whether in the physical sciences, in medicine, or in the workplace.[12] The philosophical rationale behind 'machine age' thinking goes back to the Cartesian model, which tended to assume that the way to understand anything – from literature to anatomy – was by taking it apart to identify its basic ingredients. Only then – if anything was left – would it be permissible to try and put it all back together again. Inflexible concepts of cause and effect were used to analyse everything, and a virtue was made of keeping things separate – even to the extent of constructing an artificial context for experimentation (the laboratory) where by definition the influence of the natural environment was excluded. It is little wonder that Western culture for the last few centuries has been largely fragmented and has lacked a holistic vision.

But was there more to this world view than an outmoded scientific method? This was the point at which Ackoff went further than other academics of his day, by overtly connecting the old ways of doing things with religious beliefs. He claimed that undergirding the Machine Age were two basic understandings: 'that the universe was a machine created by God to do His work, and that He had created man in His image'. This in turn led to the conclusion that 'man ought to be creating machines to do his work', and this understanding in turn led to the Industrial Revolution, which Ackoff describes as

> a consequence of man's efforts to imitate God by creating machines to do his work. The industrial organizations produced . . . were taken to be related to their creators, their owners, much as the universe was to God . . . employees were treated as replaceable machines or machine parts even though they were known to be human beings. Their personal objectives, however, were considered irrelevant by employers . . . the very simple repetitive tasks they were given to do were designed as though they were to be performed by machines.[13]

In the process, both workers and managers were dehumanized. Their personal and family life disintegrated in the face of the corporate machine and its many demands – and it was all the fault of Christianity.

In making such claims, Ackoff not only placed a question mark against the serviceability of religion in the new world order, but also promoted an alternative spirituality which would inspire and motivate the Systems Age in much the same way as he believed Christianity had provided the intellectual infrastructure for the Machine Age. Though 'many individuals find comfort in assuming the existence of . . . a unifying whole', and can call it 'God',

> This God, however, is very different from the Machine-Age God who was conceptualized as an individual who had created the universe. God-as-the-whole cannot be individualized or personified, and cannot be thought of as the creator. To do so would make no more sense than to speak of man as creator of his organs. In this holistic view of things man is taken as a part of God just as his heart is taken as a part of man.[14]

Significantly, this new 'spiritual' basis for business is then explained in terms borrowed straight from the leaders of the 1960s' Californian counter-culture, whose ideas were explored briefly in the previous chapter:

> this holistic concept of God is precisely the one embraced by many Eastern religions which conceptualize God as a system, not as an element . . . There is some hope, therefore, that in the creation of systems sciences the cultures of the East and West can be synthesized. The twain may yet meet in the Systems Age.[15]

Whether or not Ackoff intended to draw a distinction between religion as a bad thing and spirituality as the panacea for all ills, that was the natural outcome of the way he presented his ideas, especially since he also constantly referred to the coming 'new age' (albeit in lower-case letters) in a way that was certainly not inconsistent with the populist and more apocalyptic style of 1980s' 'New Age' vision represented by the likes of Marilyn Ferguson. Even though he was writing an academic text, Ackoff used unashamedly mystical imagery to define his terms of reference:

> [the coming new age] is a movement of many wills in which each has only a small part to play . . . It is taking shape before our eyes. It is still too early, however, to foresee all the difficulties that it will generate. Nevertheless, I believe the new age can be trusted to deal with them. Meanwhile there is much work to be done, much scope for greater vision, and much room for enthusiasm and optimism.[16]

This sort of language certainly has striking similarities with the media hype that was used to promote the 'Harmonic Convergence' a few years later in 1987, when an attempt was made to change the course of world events by gathering together groups of people across the world who would bring about transformation through a global festival of shamanic chanting, drumming and meditation, as a result of which 'Energy will flow through the linked network . . . as we learn to become co-creators and friends with God.'[17]

It is not difficult to challenge this understanding of Western culture. No one would dispute that the mindset which we have inherited from the Industrial Revolution – despite all its achievements – has many built-in weaknesses, not least the dehumanizing of work and workers which Ackoff so eloquently describes. But it is much more difficult to demonstrate that this is the logical outcome of the Christian belief in God as creator. Indeed, it is questionable whether religious beliefs as such have ever exercised much influence at all in the organization of the typical industrial workplace. The drawing of easy connections between simplistic religious views of God as a celestial machine-minder and the philosophy of managers is itself a good example of the over-rationalized style of thinking that characterized the so-called 'Machine Age'. Connections like this can seem to make sense in an academic atmosphere isolated from the broader concerns of real life, but they hardly ever happen in the larger context of ordinary daily experience. Most industrialists have been far too busy with other things to spend time in speculation about such concerns. The idea that the barons of the Industrial Revolution scoured books of theology looking for models of God as a way of improving efficiency and profits is just ludicrous. The majority of them only attended church irregularly, if at all, and very few claimed to be Christian in any committed sense of the word. If Ackoff's analysis was correct, we would expect Christian employers to have provided us with examples of the worst excesses of manipulation and exploitation of the workers. The reality was exactly the opposite, and those who did espouse overtly Christian values (like the Cadbury and Rowntree families in Britain) established model factories which actually reflected many of the more enlightened attitudes now being advocated by systems theorists. From today's perspective, it is easy to criticize the form of caring working community which they created as being too paternalistic and over-protective, but the very existence of Christian industrialists with that level of concern for their workers places an enormous question mark against the simplistic assumption that Christianity is the root cause of the fragmentation and disharmony which now besets the Western world.

However, industrialists generally pay little attention to history: if they think about it at all they are likely to adopt the opinion of Henry Ford, inventor of the mechanized production line, who famously declared that 'History is more or less bunk. It's tradition. We don't want tradition. We want to live in the present and the only history that is worth a tinker's damn is the history we make today.'[18] Fordism is actually a good example of what happens when the original purpose of machines is discarded, and what was intended to be a means to an end becomes the end in itself. Ackoff proposed that the ideological root of industrialization was to be found in 'man's efforts to imitate God by creating machines to do his work'[19] – but God's work always included space and time for workers to be fully human, and to be recognized and valued for their God-endowed capacities.[20] It was only when the focus moved from contemplation of God, to be exclusively focused instead on the need to make money, that work and workplaces became increasingly dehumanized. In Britain, the importance of human (and divine) values was highlighted by the emergence of labour unions, whose historic roots were in the Methodist tradition, and until the mid-twentieth century most corporations recognized the importance of caring for their workers, even if they did little to address it. But by the 1980s, other pressures were rather more urgent, and in spite of all the talk of mutual interdependence, interactive networks, and other similar high-sounding ideals deriving from systems thinking, the reality of the financial bottom line could not be avoided. While the unleashing of a new wave of global capitalism in the Thatcher-Reagan years brought riches for some, it also became a fast track to ruin for others. Successful businesses were increasingly driven by the need to beat the competition, and all manner of fancy marketing tools emerged as the way to do this. This became an open door for any experimental ideology that could find an advocate, and increasingly desperate managers began to look in the most unlikely of places to locate the magic key which would somehow open markets that had hitherto remained firmly closed. If that key could not only sell goods, but also offer increasingly stressed employees the possibility of enhancing their own inner lives at the same time, then all that was required was to identify the programme that would most effectively deliver on this promise. There was no shortage of spiritual entrepreneurs willing to do just that, and the 1980s saw a veritable explosion of such training programmes and management techniques, some of them overtly based on the ideas of people like Russell Ackoff. Names like Werner Ehrhardt, founder of the Est programme – later repackaged as The Forum – and Lou Tice of the Pacific Institute were on the lips of all the savvy managers of the day, who not only attended their seminars themselves but also promoted them throughout workforces that included government agencies as well as regular commercial enterprises. In the process, a good deal of bad press was generated both in the USA and the UK, as employees reacted with varying degrees of disbelief and despondency. The sort of complaint that made the headlines typically concerned the bullying tactics allegedly used by some of these organizations, but beneath the surface was a deeper dissatisfaction by many employees who felt that their entire world view was being questioned. In some high profile cases involving Muslims as well as believers from the Judeo-Christian tradition, it was claimed that such courses were challenging the fundamental belief systems of employees in a way that was neither benign nor objective.

I do not intend to delve any further into these particular issues, partly because I have already written about them extensively in *What is the New Age still saying to the Church*, partly also because things have moved on significantly since then. On the one hand, it has come to be widely accepted that a person's spirituality should feed into what goes on in the workplace[21] and, on the other, the more extreme examples of spiritual training which gave rise to claims of brainwashing and manipulation have largely disappeared from the scene. As part of this process, a more diversified understanding of what constitutes 'spirituality' has emerged, and it is to this wider definition that we now turn our attention.

Three snapshots of 'spirituality'

In exploring this theme, I want to take three different books (chosen more or less randomly), all of them written with a popular readership in mind. Two of them are specifically aimed at helping people to be more spiritual in their daily work, while the third includes that but also promotes spirituality as a broader lifestyle concern. They are considered here in their original order of publication, as that also will serve to identify the direction in which the trend is moving as we seek to understand the sort of things that are now regarded as spiritual.

The Executive Mystic

Barrie Dolnick's book *The Executive Mystic* was published in 1998, and is typical of one type of approach to the incorporation of spiritual values into everyday lifestyles.[22] The subtitle, 'Psychic Power Tools for Success', indicates something of what is on offer, and the author promises her readers that mastering these tools will ensure for them a glittering future:

> Psychic power tools . . . can pave the way to a better, more productive workday and a more satisfying and successful career no matter what your field . . . Psychic power tools will help you attract opportunity, maximize quality in yourself and others, counter negativity from colleagues, plan more effective meetings, make better hiring decisions, build more

> productive teams, and increase your ability to cut through the constant clutter and distraction around you.[23]

She reassures the sceptics that the book is

> not a ghost-busting guide for corporate [executives but rather] . . . a completely accessible and practical guide to getting ahead in business using intuition and other psychic power sources . . . using your psychic power will neither transform you into a late-blooming flower child nor turn you into an ardent New Ager.[24]

Judging from the commendations on the dust jacket, she has at least some satisfied readers. One, from Pete Wade, vice president and senior analyst with accountants Lehman Brothers, says, '*The Executive Mystic* really does provide an edge in business . . . especially on Wall Street. The real-world examples of deflecting negative energy are particularly useful, as is the chapter on conquering the "dark side" of psychic power.' Another, Ruth Ayres, identified as marketing director of N.W. Ayer & Partners, testifies that after following its advice, 'I received the biggest job offer of my career. This book provides information that is actionable and gets results. It's not hocus pocus – it really works!'

So what is this programme? The one thing it is not is rational: the preface advises readers that 'you must, to some degree, suspend your desire for logic and proof', advice that is reinforced in a later chapter by the recommendation to 'numb your mind'.[25] The search for personal self-understanding and the achievement of personal goals, even at the cost of perhaps persuading others to act against their own judgement, is another basic component: 'Psychic power tools can be combined in many ways to bring about smooth business interactions and help you get what you want . . . to help you influence even an unwilling audience . . . [show you] how to combine your knowledge and skills to make a powerful impression.'[26]

As aids to the pursuit of this satisfying and integrated lifestyle, readers are further advised about topics that include choosing office furniture, decorating work spaces, deciding what colour clothes to wear on different occasions, and how to defuse potentially confrontational situations. Much of this is homespun wisdom of the kind that previous generations might have taken for granted, the only difference being that here it is wrapped up in the same kind of psycho-babble as Walter Truett Anderson encountered when he attended an *Est* course, which he colourfully describes as 'some good ideas intermixed with a lot of baloney . . . sub mediocre psychotherapy and brilliant marketing'.[27]

The psychic executive is unlikely to be put off by that sort of complaint, for he or she is being offered the ability not only to overcome personal weaknesses, but to master techniques that, it is claimed, can actually change the shape of reality itself. This includes simple mind-over-matter exercises, such as trying to change your personality by changing your handwriting,[28] but goes well beyond that with the claim that 'Psychic power is the ability to sense and see beyond physical reality, to remove the barrier of time and to shift or influence events accordingly'.[29] The author gives an example of such power when she describes how this practice of 'sending energy into the future' can not only open paths through gridlocked traffic and create parking spaces where there were none, but also delay flight departures until the tuned-in executive is ready to board.[30] Whether any individual can actually achieve all this will depend on many factors. The heritage from past lives might have a bearing,[31] but more likely it will be related to the seriousness of purpose with which managers purify their space, build up their own good *karma*, are aware of their *chakras*, or know the astrological birth signs of other people in their organization. Crystals are powerful conductors of psychic energy, though they can be a mixed blessing, channeling negative energies as well as positive ones. But used wisely, they can make a significant difference to the spiritual atmosphere: 'Putting an amethyst next to your computer will help keep you feeling relaxed and at ease. Traveling with a clear quartz crystal can make a business trip seem like a breeze.'[32] Colours can be used to similar effect, along with herbs and symbolic artefacts which might range from an acorn to a gargoyle, a candle, sand, shells, or plants. The discovery of one's personal 'power animal' is of particular importance. This is a kind of spirit guide, which is to be encountered in the context of guided meditation, for which instructions are given. For those who find it hard to imagine a suitable beast, there is a long list of animals and their alleged secret powers.[33] Many other devices are also recommended, including the use of oracles to foresee future events, the Tarot, Runes, I Ching, and 'bibliomancy'.[34]

Those who are concerned about the negative influences that other colleagues might be creating should 'Sprinkle sea salt along the doorway or entryway to your workspace. This cleanses those who enter your environment.'[35] Other advice includes tuning into the cycles of the moon, carrying various amulets and charms for different situations (there is a list of items that are especially powerful in different circumstances), instructions on 'time shifting . . . [which is] the ability to make time last "longer" when you need it to, and to make time pass more quickly when you can't wait anymore.'[36] Other proposals relate more directly to the success of business propositions:

> If you are selling something, increase the desirability of your product by anointing it with an actual power scent . . . or by creating a charm with the product's name written inside it. If you are trying to protect a certain project . . . Sprinkle salt over it, then blow the salt off of it, into the wastebasket or out of the window.

When sending a project or proposal through the mail:

> You can pass a crystal over the project to increase its power . . . Bless what you are sending out either aloud or with your exhaling breath.[37]

The ideological explanation for all this is placed well beyond rational criticism by the suggestion that we can get our lives right by tuning in to cosmic powers beyond and greater than ourselves, because the correct techniques will enable the individual to access the power behind the entire universe:

> Because psychic power is much bigger than your individual power – your psychic power is hooked up to the 'cosmic hard drive' – you're endowed with the benefit of universal power, too.[38]

It is of course hard to know how seriously the average business manager regards this sort of advice, though the existence of a significant market for such books (and the courses that accompany them) suggests that more people are attracted to it than we might imagine. The continued popularity of *A Course in Miracles*, a very substantial volume that consists of messages allegedly channeled in the 1970s from cosmic masters (including Jesus Christ) by psychology professor Helen Schucman, testifies to the perpetual attraction of such ideas.[39] But we hardly need to look that far, for glossy magazines and newspapers are full of adverts for similar techniques to help people cope with the pressures of life. The one thing that we probably can say for certain is that most people who utilize such nostrums do so for purely pragmatic reasons, and it is highly unlikely that they adopt the total world view that might seem to be reflected in such books. Christians can be prone to jump to easy conclusions, seizing on one aspect or another as occult, demonic, or whatever their other current bête noire happens to be. But the reality is that a book like *The Executive Mystic* is none of these things. It is actually just a jumble of all sorts of ideas, many of which may be self-contradictory and incompatible with one another, mixed up quite uncritically without any evaluation of their source – and, one suspects, in many cases with no knowledge of their possible use or relevance in other contexts. There are just four fundamental cords binding them all together:

- a tendency towards self-indulgence, assuring hard-pressed managers that their power is greater than they thought
- a bias against rationality, assuring those same managers that most of what they have previously learned (MBAs included) is now worthless
- a lack of reality which in the end is likely to be damaging to more people than it helps, for even supposing any of this works, by definition only a minority can make it to the top of the corporate ladder, and the rest are left striving, only now in full knowledge of the fact that their failure to achieve is their own fault[40]
- and undergirding all this, of course, is the market-driven incentive to make money: the sheer novelty of these ideas

ensures it has some appeal for human resource managers who have tried everything else.

Spirituality for Dummies

This second book was first published in 2000, and though ostensibly dealing with a similar subject, it approaches it in quite a different way.[41] Unlike Barrie Dolnick, this author (Sharon Janis) tells us a little about her own spiritual pathway. Brought up as an atheist, she saw the movie *Jesus Christ Superstar* when she was fourteen years old, through which she experienced what she describes as 'an inner awakening'. As a student, she pursued this interest, which also connected with one of her major subjects of study (neurophysiology), and eventually she met Swami Muktananda and committed herself to living in the Siddha Yoga Meditation Monastic Ashram in New York state, where she stayed for ten years before moving to Hollywood to become a TV and movie producer before embarking on a career as a writer and spiritual guide.[42] During her time in the ashram, she received the name Kumuda, which she relinquished (at least in public) on her return to mainstream life in California – something she found difficult, as she explains on her website:

> In a way, I resented having to answer to this name. Sharon had been locked away long ago with all the painful childhood memories associated with her. As far as I was concerned, Sharon had been a victim, while Kumuda was spiritual and powerful. I did not want to become Sharon again.

Give or take the details, that kind of statement resonates with very many people who are searching for a meaningful spiritual identity: the desire to regain control of their lives from the cultural forces that oppress them and make them feel less than fully human.

This author's openness in making her own story so accessible is far from irrelevant for an understanding of her book, for here is a spirituality that has been tried and tested as a lifestyle involving serious commitment, and not a little self-discipline and challenge. But can anything spiritually serious be presented in the format of a *For Dummies* book? Though it includes volumes on a wide diversity of subjects, most readers come across this series as a 'how-to' guide on technical matters related to computers and other icons of modern living. Like other books in the series, this one is illustrated throughout by cartoons, complete with boxes containing 'words of wisdom' as well as things to remember and things to do. It is also accompanied by an audio CD which readers are invited to play in connection with various meditative exercises. This contains roughly equal numbers of tracks from the Judeo-Christian tradition (the Desert Fathers, as well as more contemporary Gospel music), and from the author's own interests in the Indian tradition of mystical spirituality. Reflecting on the format and presentation of the book, and the sort of technical advice offered in other volumes in the series, it struck me that 'spirituality' might perhaps be described as the software of humankind – a possibility that in turn led me to the reflections on neurotheology later in this chapter.

Whatever metaphor may be used, the book is not lacking in serious content, or in critical awareness of the questions of definition we have already mentioned in a previous chapter. It offers some reflections on the difference between religion and spirituality, suggesting that while spirituality may be included in religion, spirituality does not need to have a religious content: 'Religions usually act with a mission and intention of presenting specific teachings and doctrines while nurturing and propagating a particular way of life' while 'Spirituality relates more to your personal search, to finding greater meaning and purpose in your existence' – something that might include:

> Looking beyond outer appearances to the deeper
> significance and soul of everything
> Love and respect for God
> Love and respect for yourself
> Love and respect for everybody.

Indeed, 'Religion and spirituality can blend together beautifully!'[43]

A spiritual person is therefore someone who moves 'beyond

mere outer appearances and the five senses to an intuitive perception of the causes behind outer conditions. Someone with a spiritual approach may change and uplift their world by first transforming and improving his or her own vision.'[44] The remainder of the book is devoted to exploring how that awareness of the spiritual might be nurtured and developed. Though there is a good deal of advice on the importance of practising specific spiritual disciplines such as prayer or meditation, a good 50 per cent of the material here is focused on enhancing the experience of ordinary life – things like going to see a movie, eating wholesome food, developing an attitude of forgiveness, and much more besides. The Bible is quoted as readily as Indian religious texts, and questions about God are on the agenda without apology or embarrassment.

It would be pointless to try and pretend that this is a distinctively Christian book, but it is certainly not anti-Christian, and indeed could well repay further reflection by Christians who wish to live a life that is more grounded in God. Though the author refers to many different religious traditions, none of them are trivialized or confused with each other, nor is there anything remotely approximating to the 'quick-fix' approach that is so evident in *The Executive Mystic*. Being spiritual for Sharon Janis is serious work that needs to be rooted in some identifiable historic tradition, and demands a good deal of commitment to see it through. In this respect, it is very similar to the distance learning course, *The Quest*, produced by the Findhorn Foundation, with a careful balance being struck between taking seriously one's own experience of life at the same time as being open to learn from the wisdom of others through the centuries.[45]

The Complete Idiot's Guide to Spirituality in the Workplace

This third book is the most recent of the three, being published in 2002.[46] It is part of a series that has a very similar format to *Spirituality for Dummies* and that covers roughly similar subjects. As we might expect from its title, this particular volume deals with all the obvious topics that concern people in work: conflict and anger management, loyalty, trust, motivation, and so on. It offers advice for a whole range of practical circumstances, such as how to deal with differences between personal values and company expectations, how to deal with disciplinary matters, relating to co-workers who lose their jobs – and the perennial issue of so-called life/work balance. It is a good book, well researched, engagingly written, and full of sensible advice from an author (C. Diane Ealy) who obviously knows what she is talking about. Yet though it constantly uses terms like 'spirituality' and 'spirit wisdom' it clearly exists in a different frame of reference altogether from either of the other two. While its interests overlap to some extent with matters covered in *Spirituality for Dummies*, it has absolutely nothing at all in common with *The Executive Mystic*, and the average reader would struggle with the idea that they both deal with anything like the same subject matter. This is how *The Complete Idiot's Guide* defines what it means to be spiritual:

> Spiritual employees embody many attributes: compassion, balance between task orientation and people skills, honesty, clear boundaries with others. They are the calm in the midst of a storm, creative problem-solvers, firm and direct in their dealings with others. They avoid abusive relationships and refuse to participate in the rumor mill. Spiritual employees have their faults and make every effort to face their shortcomings.[47]

There is nothing wrong with any of that. But, as far as I can see, there is not a single reference anywhere in the book's 337 pages either to God, or to anything transcendent, or indeed to anything else that conventional wisdom might previously have identified with what it means to be spiritual. There is only one reference to religion, and that is a passing comment on the way some religious organizations function.[48]

This is fairly typical of a whole genre of recent writing on 'spirituality'. By contrast with either of the other two books, this one might be characterized as a kind of 'secular' spirituality, focused almost entirely on living the good life within a more or less materialist paradigm (using that word in a non-pejorative sense). Being spiritual is about the food we eat, the clothes we wear, the sort of attitudes we adopt, the relationships we make. Previous generations might have taken much of it for granted as the good manners of socially conscious individuals – attitudes that might indeed be characteristic of religious people but which had no intrinsic or necessary connection with any sort of belief system.

The spiritual spectrum

I am conscious of the fact that three books hardly make a library, and in an ideal world it would be worth conducting a more extensive survey of the different approaches to 'spirituality' that are out there in today's marketplace. But in this context, we will have to make do with this relatively small sample, and I will need to ask my readers to trust me when I say that I have done my homework and I have every confidence that these three examples are indeed representative of the spectrum of things that seem to be described as 'spiritual' nowadays. That being the case, I want to suggest that in response to the question about what people mean when they speak of 'spirituality' or being 'spiritual', we might offer a diagram like the following, in which 'spirituality' is not so much a single identifiable entity, as a trajectory that can be traced across the whole spectrum of human consciousness:

Lifestyle	**Discipline**	**Enthusiasm**
Values	Commitment	Experimentation
Community	Structure	Freedom
Belonging	Authority	Experience
Morality	Traditional faiths	Mystery
(*Idiot's Guide*)	(*Dummies*)	(*Executive Mystic*)

By way of unpacking the significance of some of this, I want briefly to reflect on each of these categories, paying most attention to the first of them because this is the aspect that will probably be least familiar, and certainly least self-evident to most readers.

Lifestyle spirituality

When I delivered the lectures on which this book is based, I used the term 'secular spirituality' to describe this category. On further reflection, I realized that to put 'secular' and 'spiritual' in the same phrase did not quite encapsulate what I wanted to say, nor did it reflect the deeply rooted nature of this concern in today's culture. There could of course be a further debate as to whether 'lifestyle spirituality' is the most appropriate way of describing this phenomenon, but whatever we call it there can be no doubt of its reality. It is perhaps the most widely embraced manifestation of what Linda Woodhead has variously called 'the turn to life'[49] or the 'subjective turn', which she defines as 'a turn away from life lived in terms of external or "objective" roles, duties and obligations, and a turn towards life lived by reference to one's own subjective experiences'.[50]

The most comprehensive analysis of this shift is probably that offered by Don Cupitt, in his book *The New Religion of Life in Everyday Speech*.[51] We have all become familiar with some of the ways in which it typically manifests itself. The mourning for Princess Diana in 1997 was perhaps the most high-profile example of all, in which millions of people who by reference to other indicators could be regarded as 'secular' unexpectedly and (in this case) publicly and communally expressed their anguish in ways that previously might have been regarded as the exclusive domain of conventional religious expression.[52] Shrines were constructed in public spaces as well as in homes, accompanied by the trappings of traditional devotion such as candles, incense, images, symbols, and prayers, but apparently without any underlying belief system apart from a generally expressed need to connect with other people, and a hope that such rituals might somehow transcend the sadness by relating to a larger reality. This feeling was by no means unique to that occasion, of course, and for every shrine that was created for the princess there are dozens more lining our roadsides to mark the tragic lives and deaths of others who are known only to their relatives and close friends. As Cupitt points out, the way this kind of thing might be described depends on who is doing the talking, and whereas some Christians might regard it as 'the secularization of religion' (wrongly in my opinion), it could just as easily be regarded as 'the sacralization of life'.[53] That, indeed, is how Cupitt prefers to think of it, and he argues persuasively that what would in previous generations have been a spirituality concerned with death and the next life has to a large extent been displaced by a concern for the meaningfulness of *this* life.

He proposes that this change can be discerned through the many ways in which the actual word 'life' is now used in common speech, and in order to support this view he identifies more than 140 everyday expressions which exemplify this shift of emphasis. They include such terms as 'the facts of life', 'life force', 'the kiss of life' along with exhortations like 'get a life', or 'you've got your whole life before you', concepts like 'reverence for life' or 'lifestyle', and commonly expressed sentiments such as 'taking my life in my hands', 'getting on in life', 'living life to the full', and so on.[54] He traces the way that these and similar expressions have entered everyday language only in relatively recent times, and on the basis of a careful examination of contemporary idiom he proposes that 'the recent changes in the meaning and use of the word "life" amount . . . to a major religious event',[55] at the heart of which is 'the change from a God-centred to a Life-centred religious vocabulary'.[56] Indeed, he further proposes that 'religious idioms in which we can talk about life . . . [are] now daily voiced and expressed in association with *life*, whereas their old association with *God* has suddenly and simply dropped out of living speech'[57] – a claim which he proceeds to back up by identifying fourteen separate themes in this usage which have clear parallels with traditional creedal expressions of faith, covering such topics as transcendence and immanence, mystery, holiness, conversion, providence – and even eschatology.[58]

Despite his self-deprecating assertion that 'There is no system . . . I just make it all up'[59] Cupitt's analysis has a good deal to commend it. It certainly accords with my own understanding of recent intellectual trends, which have consistently undermined the possibility of belief in any external reality to such an extent that all we now have left is ourselves. Far from representing some narcissistic, self-centred outlook, our concern with ourselves and our own lives is the inevitable outcome of a culture that has left us bereft of anything else worth believing in. But as Cupitt astutely observes, 'when people abandon traditional religious allegiance, they do not suddenly stop using religious language, having religious feelings, and thinking in religious ways'.[60] On the contrary, 'traditional belief in God cannot be just lost. It has to be replaced: and our new religious attitude to life represents a secularization of belief in God that allows us to continue using some of the old vocabulary, and expressing most of the old feelings.'[61]

This change has created the cultural matrix within which the notion of spirituality has been able to flourish in ostensibly secular settings, such as healthcare, social work, and the business world. But it permeates more than just these professional spheres, and impinges on much of everyday life as well, at least in the West (the rest of the world is a different story altogether). Encouraged by politicians as well as the media, we are all more aware of the importance of healthy lifestyles and the possibility that almost everything we touch could be toxic – the furniture in our homes, the food in our shops, the air we breathe, the cars we drive, and the way we spend our leisure time. It is easy to dismiss all these concerns as the self-indulgence of people who already have too much, and in some ways this trend can be interpreted as offering support for Maslow's notion of a hierarchy of needs, in which he postulated that spirituality ('self-actualization' in his jargon) was the ultimate goal of a materialist society.[62] His reasoning can be questioned, not least in light of the obvious fact that most of the world's people are self-evidently not materially rich, and yet generally have a more extensive interest in the spiritual (in every sense of the word) than Western populations. Indeed, many religious traditions would claim that affluence is a hindrance to spiritual enlightenment, and is to be avoided in exchange for an ascetic lifestyle. But that should not allow us to ignore the reality of this search for ways of living the good life through what I am calling here lifestyle spirituality. From a missiological perspective, the sense of emptiness, and the need to fill the spaces with something of meaning – even if it is only organic food or environmentally friendly washing powder – represents a desperate search for reality in our culture, which Christians should neither ignore nor ridicule.

The emergence of this lifestyle spirituality undoubtedly represents both a challenge and an opportunity for Christians, and much of the rest of this book will be concerned with exploring that. Actually, there is a fair amount of evidence to indicate that at least some Christians are already connecting with the search for spiritual meaning as it is being expressed in ostensibly secular terms. It is no coincidence that one of the best-selling Christian books at the start of the twenty-first century was Rick Warren's *The Purpose Driven Life*,[63] nor that the published version of the popular Alpha Course should be entitled *Alpha: Questions of Life*.[64] Indeed, a growing band of Christian writers are using the term 'life' in exactly the same way as Cupitt identifies in the wider 'secular' culture, and doing so with considerable acceptance.[65]

From a Christian perspective, it is worth noting that the writers of the Bible would find my phrase 'lifestyle spirituality' highly puzzling, if not completely meaningless. For them, it was natural to regard all the activities of everyday life as being spiritual. That is the theme of a whole section of the Hebrew scriptures, namely the wisdom literature (Proverbs, Ecclesiastes, Song of Solomon, Job) where everything from business dealings to sex is dealt with, not in terms of any sort of transcendent reality, but simply as part of the enrichment of life and the empowerment of people to be the best they can be. A similar outlook is reflected in the teaching of Jesus. In the Synoptic Gospels of Matthew, Mark, and Luke Jesus speaks extensively about 'the kingdom of God' as (among other things) a reality that impinges on such everyday things as the way people pay their taxes, relate to their families, or deal with the poor and destitute. In the fourth Gospel, John, the terminology most often adopted is that of 'eternal life' – which also seems to have an intrinsic connection with the discovery of meaning and purpose in this life in circumstances as varied as parties, picnics, and even the workings of the legal system. While it might appear that it is a twenty-first century trend to define spirituality by reference to what it is not (religion), the very same distinction was actually central to the teaching of Jesus, who regularly found himself at odds with religious people for much the same reasons as today's spiritual searchers.

Christians ought to have a distinctive contribution to offer to this widespread search for spiritual meaning in everyday life. It has often been claimed that the charismatic movement, at least in its early days, was one manifestation of this growing concern for the quality of life itself. It is certainly the case that when charismatic churches first emerged in the 1960s and 1970s, one of the things that distinguished them from traditional churches of the day was their emphasis on human potential and personal fulfilment, community, and creativity. Though many would agree with Stephen Hunt that the charismatic movement has replaced a focus on God with 'a preoccupation with religious experience and happy sing-along songs'[66] it is noteworthy that Paul Heelas and Linda Woodhead concluded their study of the spiritual life of Kendal by claiming that such congregations are the only ones likely to have much of a future.[67]

Discipline

This second type of popular spirituality is the one in which the majority of churchgoers will feel most at home, because traditional religious practice would fall into this category. But so would things like concern for keeping oneself healthy, especially when that is combined with intentional physical exercise, whether that be in the form of intense sporting activity or more gentle, but regular, pastimes like walking, cycling, or swimming. Because this kind of disciplined intentionality is likely to be familiar to most readers, I will spend correspondingly less time reflecting on it. At its best, it stands quite precisely midway between the two extremes of my spectrum. It is, if you like, 'respectable spirituality', eschewing what might be regarded as the excesses of the two ends of the spectrum, wishing to be neither focused entirely on everyday life, nor wholeheartedly enthusiastic about direct personal experience of the transcendent. In this context, the connection between God and the business of daily living might be regarded mainly as something to be acted out rather than consciously reflected upon, with personal spirituality understood in the same way, as an essentially private relationship between the individual and the divine, the details of which are unlikely to be shared easily with any other person. It is not difficult to describe this form of spirituality in derogatory and negative terms, and it does easily lend itself to becoming obsessive behaviour – whether in the gym or the church. But the truth is that this kind of faithful, disciplined practice clearly meets the spiritual needs of very many people – often in ways that others find incomprehensible, while being unable to deny the reality of it. I remember some years ago attending a memorial service for a national Christian leader in Scotland, who had died at an unexpectedly young age. Most of the service consisted of the singing of hymns, all of them traditional, many of them relics of the Moody and Sankey era of Victorian sentimentality. Virtually none of it connected with me, though looking around it was obvious that I was in a minority, and the majority of those there were not only deeply moved in an emotional sense but were also transported to some other level of consciousness that was both tangible and profoundly meaningful – if not transformational – for them. The same kind of experience appears to be generated for other people by the singing of charismatic worship songs. In evangelical churches, the very word 'worship' seems to have come to be synonymous with singing, something that other Christians find puzzling for it seems to preclude prayer, ritual, symbol – even the sacraments – from being regarded as 'worship'. The reality, though, is that in some churches singing – in whatever style – has itself become the liturgy.[68] This way of creating spiritual experiences through singing is every bit as disciplined, predictable, and ultimately controlled, as the historic forms of worship to be found in other parts of the world Church. Of course, it is precisely the discipline and control that is seen as the problem for those who regard religion as the disease and spirituality as the cure. There can be no doubt that this kind of structured spiritual expression easily slips into a McDonaldized way of articulating and addressing life's big questions.[69] But it is also the case that very many people find spiritual meaning and purpose in this, otherwise nobody at all would be in traditional churches. Moreover, the fact that discipline and commitment are key recommendations of a text like *Spirituality for Dummies* should alert us to the likelihood that these preferences for different forms of spiritual expression are perhaps related to some deep-seated realities of what it means to be human – physiological, psychological, or a mixture of the two. From a Christian angle, we should not forget that in spite of much cynicism about the way organized religion easily degenerates into empty formality, the Bible also identifies such structured observance as a gateway to experience of the numinous.

For those who practise such discipline within an overtly identified spiritual tradition, however, it is not Christian disciplines and practices which tend to have the greatest appeal. On the contrary, traditional non-western world views seem to have a particular attraction, partly because of the perception that it is Western (and therefore, historically at least, Christian) understandings of reality that have created most of the problems in the world. From a missiological angle, it does not really matter whether that understanding is altogether correct: the more important reality is that a growing number of people believe it to be, and that belief motivates their spiritual choices. One natural way of proceeding, therefore, is to reason that, if the cause of our present predicament rests in things that are modern and Western, then one way to resolve matters will be to seek solutions in spiritualities that are ancient and Eastern (or at least, not Western in the traditional sense). Many Western people are committing themselves to Eastern spiritual paths for this reason, particularly – but not exclusively – Buddhism, often in a westernized form.

Others look to first-nation beliefs for spiritual wisdom to carry us through to a better future. Long before Europeans settled in the Americas, or Australasia, these lands – and others like them – were home to ancient nations. There can be no denying that the environmentally-friendly lifestyles of these people were suppressed, often in brutal ways, and their spirituality was devalued by Western colonists who labelled it 'primitive' and 'unscientific'. With the benefit of hindsight, it now seems that Western people could have learned much from the traditional lifestyles of aboriginal peoples. Could it therefore be that by reaffirming these values that were previously discarded, the world's peoples together might find new ways to take us forward into the future? In the process, white Westerners might also expiate some of the guilt they now feel for the behaviour of their forebears. This has become a major concern, particularly for the residents of the lands whose indigenous populations were most directly affected, and in some parts of the USA young adults can often be found reconstructing the medicine wheels and other spiritual artefacts which their forebears took such delight in destroying little more than a century ago. In Europe, the search for meaningful religious practice tends to have a different focus, and here there is a fast-growing concern for rediscovering a long-lost heritage of nature-focused spirituality. Long before the spread of classical 'Western' values, articulated through the categories of Greek philosophy and spread by the power of Christendom, European countries were home to a different, arguably more spiritual world view. Should Western people not therefore be looking for answers within their own heritage, by the rediscovery and appropriation of the kind of world view that inspired and motivated their own distant ancestors? This concern accounts for the burgeoning interest in neo-paganism in its many forms, which in northern Europe is one of the fastest-growing aspects of this part of the spiritual spectrum which I am associating with discipline.[70]

Though the adoption of forms of spiritual discipline from other cultures has often been dismissed as a 'pick and mix' approach, this is not the whole story. Visionaries like David Spangler and William Irwin Thomson wholeheartedly welcome the self-conscious merging of insights from different traditions:

> this new planetary sensibility or culture will be less a thing and more a process that nourishes our creativity and wholeness and provides sustenance for building the bodies of tomorrow . . . we are reimagining our world. We are taking hunks of ecology and slices of science, pieces of politics and a sprinkle of economics, a pinch of religion and a dash of philosophy, and we are reimagining these and a host of other ingredients into something new: a New Age, a reimagination of the world . . .[71]

But others are less convinced by this approach. Carol Riddell offers a different description of the spiritual marketplace as somewhere many different possibilities may be encountered, but inviting serious commitment rather than offering a random mixture:

> It is as if we were in a market place with many stalls offering goods. Some people go to one stall to buy, others go to another. We support each other constantly, *but the path of inner transformation is ultimately a personal one. However much we may share with others, each of us has a unique path to the Self.*[72]

This more measured approach was reflected by the research of Heelas and Woodhead based in Kendal, where most people in what they term 'the holistic milieu' turned out to be committed to a single identifiable spiritual pathway rather than mixing and matching different ideas and practices.[73]

Enthusiasm

I have chosen to use the term 'enthusiasm' to describe the high energy end of the spectrum of ways in which we speak of spirituality today. I have deliberately adopted this kind of value-neutral term so as to avoid the suggestion that there is anything wrong or improper about this form of spiritual expression. It is found under many different guises, within the Christian tradition as well as elsewhere. If sociologists are correct in placing some aspects of the charismatic movement at the 'spirituality of life' end of the spectrum, then the so-called Third Wave gave them plenty of reasons for locating other aspects of it firmly within the realm of an enthusiastic, or high-energy spirituality.[74] The fact is that, for many people, nothing spiritual has happened unless it is accompanied by apparent miracles, supernatural insights, words from heaven, visions, dreams, and so on. Barrie Dolnick's book is a striking example of this, with its emphasis on the use of mystical insights to resolve life's problems. Some of her advice is virtually identical to that embraced by Christians who operate at the enthusiastic end of the scale, and her exhortations about 'sending energy into the future' so that previously non-existent parking spaces might open up would not be out of place in some church circles I have experienced. Despite that, however (or maybe because of it), this is the bit of the 'spiritual' spectrum where most Christians begin to feel a little uneasy. For those brought up in the Reformed tradition, with its historic insistence that anything mystical was restricted to the biblical era, dismissing such claims is a matter of theological conviction. Others, who are uneasy with the notion of the *missio Dei* (that God is at work in this world), regard with suspicion any form of spiritual enthusiasm that is different from their own, and often dismiss it as a sign that dark powers are at work. But the majority still live under the shadow of a Cartesian world view that found it impossible to countenance the prospect that there might be any reality that would be non-material or non-rational in nature. At the same time, there is an uneasy awareness that enthusiasm of this sort has played a significant part in the historic Christian tradition, not only in the experience of mystics down through the centuries but also in the Bible, where there are narratives telling how Moses met God at the burning bush (Exodus 3:1-6), how Jacob encountered angels as he rested on a pillar of stone (Genesis 28:10-17) – not to mention Ezekiel's claims to have been 'lifted up between earth and heaven' so as to be able to see both Babylon and Jerusalem (Ezekiel 8:1-4), or indeed St Paul's account of a similar experience in which he was 'caught up to the third heaven' (2 Corinthians 12:2-4). While this sort of high energy spirituality does not appeal to everyone, significant numbers of people are attracted by it, whether it be offered through drumming, or therapies such as reiki or rebirthing, or through encounters with angels, or indeed through phenomena such as 'slaying in the spirit' or the Toronto Blessing in charismatic church circles.

Being human and being spiritual

I have deliberately chosen to survey and describe these various definitions of what it means to be spiritual in a phenomenological or empirical way that would identify what is going on, rather than make value judgements about it all. I know from long experience that this can create problems for Christian readers, who often want to pass judgement before hearing what others are saying. We will return to this question towards the end of the chapter. At this stage of the discussion, however, it is worth pointing out that just because something is labelled 'spiritual' does not mean it will automatically be good. Before coming back to that, I want to move on to another question, prompted by the sheer diversity of the spirituality spectrum that I have identified here. If people regard all these quite different things as being 'spiritual', what is the common thread that makes their self-definition plausible?

It was the pioneering work of William James on *Varieties of Religious Experience*[75] that first cleared the way for scientific interest in the nature of spirituality. Carl Gustav Jung's interest is well known, and his approach to understanding human nature was overtly spiritual, inspired to a significant extent by his fascination with ancient Gnosticism and his understanding of its myths as paradigms of the human condition.[76] We have already indicated how pioneering psychotherapists went on to identify the possibility that what had previously been thought of as religious experiences could be explored in purely secular, person-centred ways, and in the process created the atmosphere within which the redefinition of 'spirituality' could take place. But they were not the only ones to be attracted to this subject, and by the second half of the twentieth century empirical scientists had begun to carry out research into the nature of spirituality. In his Gifford Lectures on Science, Natural History and Religion delivered in the University of Aberdeen in sessions 1963–4 and 1964–5, Sir Alister Hardy raised the possibility that spirituality might have some intrinsic connection with human physiology – a hypothesis that he subsequently explored at his Oxford Centre for the Study of Religious Experiences.[77] Richard Bucke also proposed a similar connection, this time relating it to the evolutionary principle. He argued that evolution itself had occurred in three distinct stages: first, the evolution of consciousness (in animals), then the evolution of self-consciousness (in humans), and finally the evolution of what he called 'cosmic consciousness'. He described this 'cosmic consciousness' in a typically optimistic 1960s' counter-cultural way, but it clearly relates to the development of spirituality.[78] Meanwhile, social scientist Peter Berger had also come up with the suggestion that the construction of human culture itself is driven by a need for 'instinctual structure' in such a way that 'The world-building activity of man [sic] . . . is the direct consequence of man's biological constitution.'[79] Since spirituality (by whatever definition) is inextricably bound up with culture, then the next obvious question to ask is, how is spirituality related to biology? Some theologians – most notably Karl Barth and his followers – would regard that as an exceedingly silly question, because they see a complete separation between what can be discerned from nature and what God imparts in self-revelation, with the latter being the only thing that really matters for any genuine Christian faith.[80] This is neither the time nor the place to engage in a longer discussion about the understanding of Christian theology that lies behind this position, except to say that from a missiological angle it leads to a disengagement from some of the most important apologetic questions of our day with regard to fundamental questions about existence and identity. In particular, I do not believe it is possible to offer any sort of meaningful explanation of faith by ignoring the way in which neuroscience is now redefining the terms of reference within which we can talk of what it means to be human. In this book, it is possible to do little more than scratch the surface of this issue, which is why I have chosen to remain closely focused on how it might affect our perception of what it means to be spiritual, in the hope of setting up some helpful signposts to some aspects of the subject, even if there will be many loose ends left lying about that will impinge on other aspects of Christian belief about the nature and purpose of humankind.

In recent years, the nature of the questions, as well as the range of possible answers, has been both transformed and informed by new understandings about the nature and workings of the brain, which has inspired a whole new discipline dedicated to this phenomenon, now commonly known as neurotheology. The rising level of interest in this topic can be judged from the fact that at the time when I delivered the lectures on which this book is based (November 2004) an Internet search came up with about 3000 entries, and by the time I was completing the book, only three months later, the number had risen to 10,000. Much of the ongoing research is reported via websites, though there are some published accounts, three of which I will refer to here, each of which approaches the subject from a slightly different angle.

The biology of belief

One of the most accessible is Andrew Newberg's book *Why God won't go away*, subtitled *Brain science and the biology of belief*.[81] Andrew Newberg is a radiology professor at the University of Pennsylvania who teamed up with his late colleague, neurologist Eugene D'Aquili, to inaugurate a series of experiments in which they would use a SPECT camera to try and identify what happens in the brain when individuals are having what they would regard as 'spiritual experiences'.[82] The particular people whom they tested were a group of (Western) meditators in the Tibetan Buddhist tradition, and a group of Franciscan nuns at prayer. Newberg's analysis and interpretation of the findings is of necessity complex and loaded with neurological jargon, and there is not the space to explain it fully here. Put simply, he discovered that the frontal lobe of the brain (seat of concentration and attention) and the limbic system (where powerful emotions are processed) exhibited greater signs of activity in proportion to the depth of the spiritual experience his subjects believed they were having. Moreover, in tandem with the increased energy released in these locations, the parietal lobe exhibited symptoms of a close-down. Since this is the part of the brain in which the boundaries of the individual self are experienced, when it closes down the subject has a feeling of being part of a much bigger whole: God, or the cosmos. There is of course a lot more to it than that somewhat simplified version. But Newberg's conclusion is clear enough, even to those who might be amateurs in this field. Rejecting the Cartesian dualism between brain and mind or soul, he regards the human person as a unity in which 'mind needs brain, brain creates mind, and . . . the two are essentially the same entity, seen from different points of view.'[83] On this basis, it is scientifically accurate to say that, whatever else one might claim about spiritual experience, it must by definition involve a neurological process, whose activity can be traced through the pathways of the brain. Though he acknowledges that it would be possible to argue from this that 'religious experience is only imagined neurologically, that God is physically "all in your mind"', he dismisses this possibility and suggests that 'a full understanding of the way in which the brain and mind assemble and experience reality suggests a very different view'.[84] He illustrates his point by comparing the likely results of a SPECT scan carried out while the subject eats an apple pie. It would be possible to claim that eating the pie is 'all in the mind', since the total experience of smell, taste, touch and sight would (just like prayer or meditation) appear on a brain scan as a series of coloured blotches. But we all know 'that doesn't mean the pie is not real, or that it is not delicious' – and, in the same way, 'tracing spiritual experience to neurological behaviour does not disprove its realness'.[85] To summarize what then becomes a long and complex presentation of evidence and argument, Newberg concludes that there is no empirical justification for regarding spiritual experiences as in any way less real to the brain than any other information it receives and processes, including perceptions of the material world and everyday life:

> If you were to dismiss spiritual experience as 'mere' neurological activities, you would also have to distrust all of your own brain's perceptions of the material world. On the other hand, if we do trust our perceptions of the physical world, we have no rational reason to declare that spiritual experience is a fiction that is 'only' in the mind.[86]

While acknowledging that in some mental states the brain can of course be deceived, he insists that spiritual experiences 'are not necessarily the result of emotional distress or neurotic delusion or any pathological state at all . . . [but are] produced by sound, healthy minds coherently reacting to perceptions that in neurobiological terms are absolutely real.'[87] Indeed, he adduces evidence from several studies to demonstrate that,

> in general, . . . spiritual experiences are associated with higher-than-average levels of overall psychological health, expressed in terms of better interpersonal relationships, higher self-esteem, lower levels of anxiety, clearer self-identity, an increased concern for others, and a more positive overall outlook on life[88]

– statements which, from a Christian perspective, bear a remarkable resemblance to both the Beatitudes (Matthew 5:3-12) and St Paul's list of the fruits of the Spirit (Galatians 5:22-6).

Though (wisely in my opinion) he stops short of claiming this as any sort of proof for, say, the existence of God, Newberg's insistence on the essential trustworthiness of human intuition about what is real and what is not leads to a conclusion that undergirds the reality of what our common sense (which, in the end, is the basis for the spectrum of the spiritual that I outlined earlier) tells us: 'our understanding of the brain and the way it judges for us what is real argues compellingly that the existence of an absolute higher reality or power is at least as rationally possible as is the existence of a purely material world.'[89] Newberg's work is of particular interest because it correlates with other research into human personality and spirituality carried out from within other disciplines, and using different methodologies. His understanding of our neurological makeup correlates well with research carried out by David Hay, particularly his ethnography of spiritual experiences published as *Understanding the spirituality of those who don't go to church.*[90]

A God gene?

More recently, molecular biologist Dean Hamer has advanced this discussion even further with his book *The God Gene: how Faith is hardwired into our genes.*[91] This is another study based on empirical research, this time on a much larger sample than Newberg was able to use. Hamer is chief of gene structure at the US National Cancer Institute, and he was able to use data gained in the course of a study of smoking and addiction which collected information from more than a thousand men and women. By using a personality test devised by psychiatrist Robert Cloninger, which includes a way of measuring self-transcendence ('spirituality'), he ranked these subjects on a scale covering a wide spectrum from the least to the most spiritually inclined, and then looked for commonalities in their genes.[92] While accepting that spirituality (supposing it can be measured at all) is unlikely to be located in just one gene, his results soon pointed to a variation in a particular gene that seemed to correlate with where people were placed on the self-transcendence aspect of Cloninger's Temperament and Character Inventory. The gene was VMAT2 (so-called because it is the vesicular monoamine transporter), and depending on whether it was the nucleic acid cytosine or adenine that was found in a particular place, the self-transcendence test revealed them to be highly spiritual (cytosine) or less so (adenine). Like Newberg, Hamer also insists that his work does not lead to a reductionist attitude toward faith or spiritual beliefs. Indeed, they both in different ways argue that our ability to experience transcendence in this way is part and parcel of human evolutionary development: people with a connection to the spiritual live longer and happier.

Spiritual chemistry

The third piece of research which I will mention here is (like the other two) firmly rooted in the biomedical model of research, though the interpretation of the scientifically demonstrable findings moves in a more speculative direction. This is the work of Rick Strassman, published in his book *DMT: the Spirit Molecule.*[93] Strassman, who is a psychiatry professor at the University of New Mexico School of Medicine, approaches spiritual experiences by way of the chemical influences that he believes effect the sort of changes in brain patterns that can be tracked by the methodologies adopted by researchers like Newberg. Most specifically, he identifies DMT (N,N-dimethyltryptamine) as 'the spirit molecule' that is responsible for 'initiating or supporting mystical and other naturally occurring altered states of consciousness'.[94] DMT is a hallucinogenic drug found in various plants and also produced naturally in the body in small quantities (it is chemically related to serotonin, a basic neurotransmitter that is known to affect behaviour[95]). He carried out clinical experiments on the effects of this with more than sixty volunteers over a five-year period.

Some of his proposals are no more than informed guesses, though their correlation with other hard research makes them all the more tantalizingly attractive. Noting that this 'spirit molecule' appears to be located and produced in the pineal gland, and that this is the very place that Descartes identified as 'the seat of the soul',[96] he speculates that DMT may be produced naturally by the body in large quantities at crucial times when the physical and the spiritual connect. Such times would be especially clustered around life and death, and by connecting this idea with other research into near-death experiences, Strassman proposes that the pineal may be regarded as 'an antenna or lightning rod for the soul'[97] literally providing a route of passage whereby whatever it is that distinguishes the human person can both enter and leave the body. This becomes for him an all-embracing explanation of human nature, leading him to speculate that since the pineal gland becomes visible in a human foetus at seven weeks (roughly the same time at which the sex of a foetus also becomes apparent), this might also be the point at which a human embryo becomes a person, by virtue of having a 'spirit' or 'soul'.[98] Indeed, he proposes that the pineal produces DMT in large quantities

> at extraordinary times in our lives . . . It provides us with the vehicle to consciously experience the movement of our life-force in its most extreme manifestations . . . at birth, the pineal releases more DMT . . . mediates the pivotal experiences of deep meditation, psychosis, and near-death experiences. As we die, the life-force leaves the body through the pineal gland, releasing another flood of this psychedelic spirit molecule.[99]

As if this were not enough, Strassman eventually proposes on the basis of his research findings that DMT actually gives us real-time access to parallel universes. I have already indicated that Strassman's conclusions (though not his underlying methodology) are more tendentious than either Newberg or Hamer. But it may be (as he indeed argues) that a methodology that moves beyond the biomedical model to take account of psychological and spiritual factors could produce a more holistic final account of the chemical processes to which he has drawn attention.

Being spiritual and being Christian

Let me now pull some of this together to explain why I think it is relevant to our concerns here from a Christian perspective. The implication of studies such as these is that being spiritual is not exclusively a Christian – or even a religious – activity: it is a human activity. This is certainly the assumption behind current moves to establish spiritual care within healthcare provision and social work policies: that spirituality is a common human experience, and religion is what happens when the experience is codified into ways of life, systems of morality, cognitive beliefs, and so on. This realization seems to me to open up a series of fresh possibilities and challenges when it comes to being Christian as well as being spiritual. Theologically, this corresponds very closely to the notion of the *missio Dei*, to which reference has already been made, that is the belief that this is God's world, and God is therefore at work in it, unilaterally as it were, without the need for human agencies or intermediaries. A similar notion can be expressed using Jesus' favourite terminology of the kingdom of God, for it has long been recognized that one can be in the kingdom without also being in the church (something that used to be little more than a theological conundrum but which has a new missiological urgency in a situation where increasing numbers of people are now leaving the church in order to continue faithful following of Jesus). It also gives new meaning to statements such as that from Augustine (354–430), who famously said that 'You have made us for yourself, O God, and our hearts are restless till they rest in you.'[100] Even that was not altogether original to him, for centuries earlier the writer of Ecclesiastes had declared that '[God] has put eternity into the hearts of all, yet they cannot fathom out what God has done from the beginning to the end' (3:11). Substitute 'brains' or 'genes' or 'molecules' for 'heart' and the twenty-first-century exponents of neurotheology seem to be saying much the same thing. And, of course, we can cross-reference the entire discussion back to Genesis 1:26-7, and the statement that women and men are made 'in God's image'.

Asking questions

The ease with which we can connect this work to central concerns within the historic and orthodox Christian faith should not mask the fact that some questions are left unanswered by the sort of analysis offered by these researchers. There is a developing debate among theologians about the implications of neurotheology for Christian anthropology, though from the scientific side it is worth pointing out that both monistic and dualistic understandings of human persons have been proposed by the researchers mentioned here – and, of course, the same division of opinion can be found among Christians.[101] I do not intend to engage with that discussion here, because to do so might easily direct attention away from the main focus of this book, which is unapologetically missiological. From this perspective, I do however have some questions arising from the neurotheological insights. One of the most basic and obvious issues relates to someone who suffers damage either to those parts of the brain where spirituality is experienced (Newberg), or whose genetic makeup disposes them to be less 'spiritual' than someone else (Hamer), or whose body is deficient in DMT production (Strassman). Can such persons still have a spiritual connection?[102] Another concerns the relationship between rational reflection and spiritual experience. Because of the way they prioritize experience, all three tend to play down the distinctiveness of different religions in a way that does not match the perceptions of most religious people themselves. Newberg in particular seems to be attracted to the possibility that by getting back to the primal spiritual experience, stripped of its religious connotations, we can find some common core of human nature that will result in greater understanding among peoples that will enhance international co-operation and lead to world peace. It seems wildly optimistic to imagine that if we were all to become mystics, the world would suddenly be put to rights. But more importantly if, as Newberg also repeatedly emphasizes, we are to trust human intuition as a way of establishing the reality of what we experience in our brains (whether that be food, sex, or spirituality), then we need to extend the same trust to people in terms of their understanding of their own belief systems. While it may have seemed plausible in the 1960s to regard all belief systems as variants of one underlying reality, the possibility of doing so has receded into the far distance in the early years of the twenty-first century.

Having said that, I believe that these insights into the nature of those experiences which we label 'spiritual' point the way to understanding what the connection might be between the three main areas on the spectrum that I have identified here. Could it be that for those who identify predominantly with the lifestyle or ostensibly secular end of the spectrum, engagement with quality of life in its many manifestations is what offers that sense of fulfilment and purpose that can be tracked through neural impulses along the pathways in the brain which Newberg identifies as spiritual? At the same time, others perhaps experience the same neural impulses through what look like more conventional forms of personal discipline, whether prayer, hymns, or other aspects of traditional devotion – or indeed, commitment to the rigours of sports training, which by any definition is a spiritual experience for many.[103] And is there a third group whose sense of connection with the transcendent is mediated predominantly through high-energy experiences such as out-of-body experiences, visions, channeling, dreams, miraculous healings, or speaking in tongues? There need not be an inflexible demarcation between these various categories, and indeed it is easy to think of cases of obvious crossover from one to the other: while regular sports training might qualify as being predominantly about discipline, nobody would wish to deny that the ecstasy of doing really well – or of supporting a team that beats all the competition – would more obviously belong in the enthusiastic section of the spiritual spectrum.[104] Before this suggestion could be proposed with any sense of certainty, a lot more empirical research would be required, especially in relation to what I have called lifestyle spirituality. Speaking personally, though, I can recall occasions in my own life when ostensibly secular experiences of things like relationships, community, food, and so on have invoked the same sense of connection with God that I have at other times experienced through either structured religious practice or high-energy enthusiasm.

Harmful spirituality?

If this proposal is anywhere remotely near the mark, how then does it connect with being a Christian? Strassman concludes from his experimental data that 'The spirit molecule is neither good nor bad, beneficial nor harmful, in and of itself. Rather, set and setting establish the context and the quality of the experiences to which DMT leads us.'[105] I briefly commented earlier that spiritual experiences can be damaging as well as uplifting, and now is the time to unpack that in more detail. It seems clear that the 'buzz' which people identify as a spiritual experience – whether at the lifestyle, discipline, or enthusiasm bits of the definitional spectrum – can be described (though not fully explained) through the sort of research just mentioned. In the light of that, it is not difficult to see why different individuals and societies can apply the label 'spiritual' to so many apparently disparate experiences. But merely calling something spiritual is no guarantee that it will be good, and it is emphatically not the case that every world view that is based on a spiritual understanding will be life-giving and personally empowering. It is not difficult to find examples of spirituality leading to negative and, in some cases, destructive consequences. For example, though religion is now regularly depicted as being authoritarian and personally damaging, the processes and bureaucratic practices found in many parts of the corporate world (often dressed up to look 'spiritual') can be just as problematic as some of the abuses perpetrated in the name of religion. Indeed, they can be more damaging, if only because they are harder to challenge. In spite of all the hurt that has been caused over the centuries in the name of Christ, the reality is that it has also been challenged by other Christians, and that challenge has been possible because built into the entire Christian tradition is the consciousness that in the end we are all responsible to a higher power than ourselves, namely God. For centuries, racist oppression was justified by European Christians on the basis of a spirituality drawn from the Bible, and those who instigated the apartheid regime in South Africa only carried to a logical conclusion things that were widely believed by other Christians. But it was Christians who were instrumental in challenging that understanding, and in the end making a difference. When accountability is defined in purely human terms, that is unlikely to happen, and for that reason much of the spirituality that is being espoused in the corporate world is not offering freedom but imposing frightening levels of control that leave individuals at the mercy of power-hungry executives. Though the magnitude of his crimes placed him in a different league altogether, Adolf Hitler offers a good example of what can happen when spiritual experiences are divorced from moral accountability. He was profoundly influenced by ideas that are still embraced in some circles today, especially the notion that it might be possible to change the shape of reality itself through ritual and psychic activities.[106] The Ku Klux Klan also consists of deeply 'spiritual' people, while the destructive and disempowering impact of 'spirituality' in Irish society is so well documented as to require no further comment – not to mention ouija boards and the like. But the dark side of this search for spiritual experience is not restricted to activities with an overtly mystical overtone, for exactly the same potential for good or ill can be found in forms of spiritual discipline that have no connection at all with belief systems or faith traditions. Sports training can enhance health and physical fitness, but it can also injure and, when carried to obsessive extremes, rupture relationships and even lead to premature death. The same thing is true of mind-altering drugs.

From a Christian perspective, it is very easy to turn all this into a battle between 'them and us', and many Christians do, as we shall see in the next chapter. There is no question that the caution given by Jesus about 'false messiahs and false prophets' (Matthew 24:24) and the importance attached by Paul to the spiritual gift of discernment (1 Corinthians 12:10), are highly relevant here. But discerning what is going on in today's world is a lot more complex and challenging than a simple dualistic world view would imply. A striking example of this blew up while I was writing this book, in relation to the conduct of the Iraq war by the US military. In mid February 2005, James Mattis, a three-star general in the US Marine Corps, was taking part in a televised panel discussion and said that soldiers enjoyed shooting people. His actual words were, 'it's quite fun to fight them . . . It's a hell of a hoot . . . It's fun to shoot some people. I'll be right up there with you. I like brawling.' Not surprisingly, he was rebuked for these remarks by the Marine commandant, General Michael Hagee, and the entire episode provoked extensive discussion in the media. Though it was not explicitly claimed that killing people was also a spiritual experience, the language used clearly implied that soldiers get a buzz out of it, which on today's broad definitions of the spiritual almost certainly means that killing can be placed somewhere on that spectrum. Actually, there is no need to justify that association because there have been other examples of the same thing, most notably and notoriously the murder of actress Sharon Tate and her friends in 1969 at the hands of Charles Manson and his associates, who claimed to have committed the crime for specifically spiritual purposes. Suicide pacts entered into for explicitly spiritual reasons are open to the same understanding, and it is not altogether implausible to suppose that the buzz which soccer hooligans get out of violence would also register as brain activity in the same way. For the most part, this particular episode passed unnoticed as yet another unfortunate consequence of the invasion of Iraq in 2003. But in the US Christian press, it generated some considerable debate, not least because in an article entitled 'Onward Christian Soldiers' Gene Edward Veith asked, 'Should a Christian soldier take pleasure in killing people?' and answered that 'there is a pleasure in battle', recommending his readers to 'appreciate our troops' facility in fulfilling their purpose, namely, killing the enemy.'[107] Having counselled that 'soldiers . . . should go forward with joy', he concluded by affirming that 'As in other vocations, so in the military, there is nothing wrong with enjoying one's work.' Not all soldiers report their experiences in this optimistic way, but since 'enjoying one's work' is frequently regarded as a spiritual matter, at the lifestyle end of the spectrum, this raises some interesting questions about discernment.

Martin Marty, recognizing that the use of the phrase 'a hell of a lot of fun' seems to point to some sort of spiritual high being experienced while doing the shooting, articulated some of the most obvious questions, as follows:

> If a Christian believes that humans are made in the image of God, should it be 'a hell of a lot of fun to shoot them'? World Wars I and II, and many other wars, had Christian fighting Christian, sometimes because they were drafted to do so against their will. If a Christian believes that another Christian is a child of God, should it be a 'hell of a lot of fun to shoot' and kill him? If a Christian is an evangelical – like those to whom *World* magazine is directed – and he must kill someone who is as yet unevangelized, thus cutting short his potential for salvation, should it be a 'hell of a lot of fun' to

> shoot him? If a Christian is a grandson, son, father, husband, brother who knows that survivors of his killed counterpart will suffer all their lives because of his necessary act of killing, should it still be a 'hell of a lot of fun' to shoot him? If a Christian is to pay special attention to the weak, and he decides that someone 'ain't got no manhood left anyway' [another turn of phrase used by the general] should he do Darwin's work and eliminate the unworthy, taking a 'hell of a lot of fun' in doing it? Can the unconvinced . . . at least ask how finding it a 'hell of a lot of fun to shoot' those who 'ain't got no manhood' squares in any way with 'love your enemies'?[108]

The argument here is not about just war theories or military operations per se but about the connection between 'fun' (spiritual high) and killing, and the question is: just because a person feels good about something, does that make it right? And if having a spiritual buzz is open to misuse, how can we discern the difference between good and bad spirituality?

Telling the story

Andrew Newberg himself offers a fruitful line of reflection that I believe helps us to see not only the ethical but also the missiological significance of all this, for one of his most fascinating chapters concerns the place of ritual in relation to spiritual experience. Like an older generation of theological scholars, he makes a direct connection between ritual and story:[109]

> This is the primary function of religious ritual – to turn spiritual *stories* into spiritual *experience*; to turn something in which you believe into something you can feel . . . The neurobiology of ritual . . . turns these ideas into felt experiences, into mind-body, sensory, and cognitive events that 'prove' their reality. By giving us a visceral taste of God's presence, rituals provide us with satisfying proof that the scriptural assurances are real.[110]

This seems to me to be of crucial importance, both in understanding the spirituality of those who are not Christian, and in reflecting on an appropriate Christian engagement with today's spiritual search. The following diagram helps to explain it further:

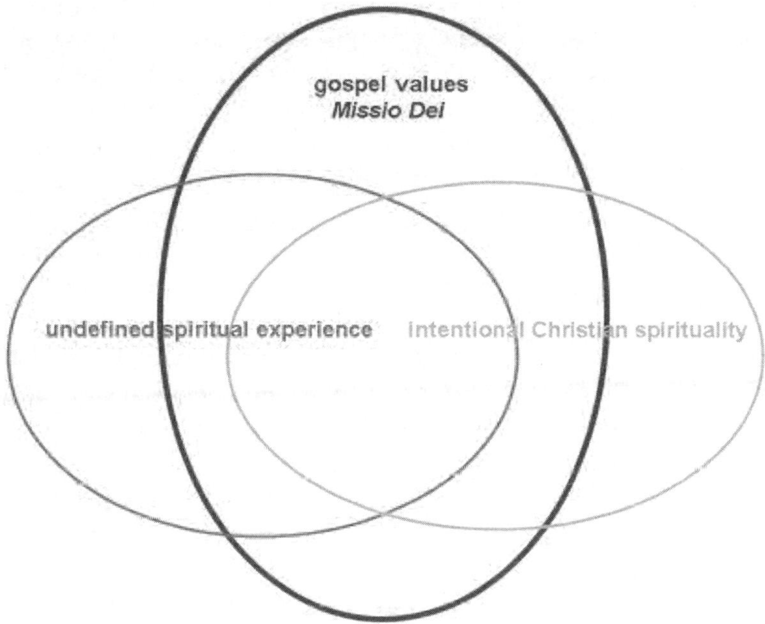

What is this saying? The foundational assumption here is that the ultimate arbiter of spiritual experience is constituted by gospel values. There is also here an acknowledgement that by virtue of being human and 'made in God's image', not only do we all have the potential for spiritual experiences that are genuinely of God, but that we all do actually have them. Implied, though not indicated on the diagram, is the assumption that these experiences will correspond to the spectrum of the spiritual previously outlined. In the case of what is called here 'intentional Christian spirituality', these experiences are recognized and named as such, whereas in the case of 'undefined spiritual experience' God in Christ may well be at work, but goes unrecognized. Furthermore, both Christians and those who are not Christian can indulge in forms of behaviour that may well count as being spiritual on a purely biological definition, but which can also be contrary to the will of God.

From a missiological angle, one other thing to notice here is that there are many forms of intentional spiritual search being practised today which have no conscious connection with any bigger story, whether Christian or otherwise, religious or not. In other words, for many people there are no foundational principles such as are indicated here by the use of the term 'gospel values'. To use Newberg's terminology, the connection between ritual and story is often lacking. The very absence of such a story is symptomatic of the situation of Western culture today, and in a world increasingly dominated by global capitalism the same thing is likely to occur in other cultures as well, because multinational corporations thrive on the hope that their own metanarrative of prosperity through purchase and possession will displace all others. This in turn tends to produce a default position in which we adopt a metanarrative focused only on the self, and what was once the normative connection between story and ritual is broken, to be replaced with a pragmatism in which rituals have neither meaning nor purpose beyond the immediate moment. Almost all the spiritually intentional disciplines being practised today under the guise of New Spirituality originally developed in the context of particular stories, but they are now being wrenched out of place and in the process their true worth is diminished. As Starhawk has so eloquently expressed it: those who are spiritually starved in their own culture 'unwittingly become spiritual strip miners, damaging other cultures in their superficial attempts to uncover their mystical treasures . . .'[111]

At the same time, it is clear that increasing numbers of people are indeed having spiritual experiences that are entirely consistent with the Christian story. The results of David Hay's research are a good example of that: though, by definition, his respondents were chosen specifically because they did not go to church (or synagogue, mosque, etc.), none of the experiences they report would be at all out of place within the mainstream of orthodox Christian belief and practice. Moreover, he reports experiences that cover the entire spectrum as I have described it here. While I was delivering these lectures in London, I heard from a Christian group who had taken a stand at a large psychic fair. Alongside their stand was one operated by a woman who specialized in angels. The centrepiece of her display on this occasion had been a painting of what she described as the most beautiful angel she had ever seen. She had received this in a vision while driving her car, along with the following message: 'I am THE LIGHT OF THE WORLD. Look into my Heart and there you will find your True Love . . . Is it not the most beautiful thing? Look into my Heart, and I will bring you Home . . . Look into my Heart and recognize that you have been there all the time . . . you within me, I within you . . . PERFECT and DIVINE.' On arriving home, she painted the picture of the angel and wrote down this message. This woman had never read the Bible or been to a church service, and was completely unaware of the fact that Jesus was known as 'the light of the world' (John 8:12). Nor did she have any prior understanding of the Eucharistic liturgy and the scriptural connotations of Christ being in us, and us being in Christ. Yet both the image and the message had close parallels with some of the most distinctive teaching of the Fourth Gospel.

From my own experience, I could multiply stories like that many times over. But because people are unaware of the Christian story – either because they have never heard it, or because they have only encountered corrupted and damaging versions of it – experiences like this simply float in a vacuum as a valuable though ultimately perplexing aspect of human experience. Alongside this, the default position of many Christians is to assume that any spiritual experience which does not explicitly name the name of Christ must therefore be unauthentic, bogus, and quite probably damaging, even perhaps demonically inspired. The advice offered by C.S. Lewis on this topic is still worth pondering:

> We must not be nervous about 'parallels' and 'pagan Christs': they *ought* to be there – it would be a stumbling block if they weren't. We must not, in false spirituality, withhold our imaginative welcome. If God chooses to be mythological . . . shall we refuse to be *mythopathic*? For this is the marriage of heaven and earth: Perfect Myth and Perfect Fact: claiming not only our love and obedience, but also our wonder and delight . . .[112]

As Lewis himself so eloquently demonstrated through his own writings, when interpreted with flair and creativity, the story of Jesus can indeed address the archetypal concerns of today's people, not least because it offers a frame of reference within which the reality of suffering and evil can be addressed. In my experience this is something that is singularly lacking from other stories currently on offer in the world of New Spirituality. The most appropriate Christian response to this discussion will therefore be to ponder how the Christian story might be offered as a resource that will not only shed light on the many understandings of spirituality held by today's spiritual searchers, but will also create an opportunity for people to journey with Jesus in the sort of experimental discipleship to which he invited his earliest followers. This will be a challenge to those churches which have lost sight of the empirical basis of their faith, and which might be inclined to agree with the opinion of New Spirituality guru Shirley Maclaine, that 'it all seems to be about feeling, not thinking . . .'[113] Meaningless experience is not, of course, the prerogative of any one tradition of the Church, and it makes little difference whether the empty ritual is enacted against a sacramental, Reformed, or charismatic background. Andrew Newberg's comment is especially relevant here, since he is not a preacher: 'If the rhythms of ritual don't generate the proper autonomic and emotional responses, the ceremony will lose its underlying power . . .'[114] Or, to express it differently, we should be making people feel so much that they can't help thinking.

There is also, however, a challenge to those others who insist that discipleship is primarily a rational, cognitive affair, and who prioritize the acceptance of doctrinal propositions unrelated to any kind of spiritual experience, whether that experience be sacramental or personal. In this connection, it is appropriate to remind ourselves of the response offered by Jesus in reply to a question about the meaning of discipleship. Quoting from the Hebrew scriptures, he reminded his questioners of something they already knew: 'Love the Lord your God with all your heart, with all your soul, with all your mind, and with all your strength . . . and Love your neighbour as you love yourself' (Mark 12:30-1). This statement coheres remarkably well not only with the insights presented through neurotheology, but also the descriptions of a whole person offered by Carl Gustav Jung. It can become an appropriate text not only for mission among spiritual searchers but also for renewed forms of ministry within a post-modern church. Unpacking the further significance of these two topics – mission and ministry – will constitute the subject matter of the rest of this book.

3 New Spirituality and Christian Mission

In the previous chapter we surveyed the cultural scene by adopting a very broad definition of what 'spirituality' might mean for today's people. There is no doubt that the wide spectrum adopted there is true to the varied ways in which words like 'spiritual' are now being used. But the reality is that not everyone wants to be spiritual by any of these definitions. Though there is indeed a widespread recognition that spirituality (by any definition) is something that can enrich many aspects of daily life, there is a difference between people who encounter the spiritual by default, and those who are intentional about seeking out spiritual encounters or experiences. Such intentionality can be found at all points on the spectrum, including the lifestyle end. For many people, the enjoyment of food is a key experience that they would describe as spiritual. It is not uncommon to find restaurants advertising their services as a holistic experience that will nurture the spirit as well as feeding the body. One of my favourite restaurants is The Little Door in Los Angeles, where the proprietor intentionally blesses the tables and those who will eat at them, as well as the staff who will serve, by wafting smouldering bunches of sage over them just prior to opening time. This practice (known as 'smudging') originated in a cleansing ritual within the native American healing tradition, but is now widely used in much the same way as incense in historic Christianity. I remember the very first time I went there: the opening blessing created an incense-filled atmosphere, and the waiter brought to our table unannounced a bowl of oil, a loaf of bread, and a bottle of wine. Was it sacramental – or just coincidence? I have no idea, but for those of us who were there these apparently bland ritual actions certainly became sacramental, because for us they connected with a bigger story with which we were familiar, recalling key elements of Christian devotion (Chrism and Eucharist). It was a good example of the importance of story, to which attention was drawn in the previous chapter – and to which we will return.

However, intentionality in seeking out the spiritual is more often manifested (or perhaps more easily recognized) at the other points on the spectrum – what I have called the disciplined and the enthusiastic. The discipline might as easily be focused on the maintenance of good health, or achievement in sports, as in religious devotion, whether Christian or some other – and the enthusiasm likewise. It is no coincidence that health clubs have grown like mushrooms in the night at the same time as churches have gone into decline – nor that people who are concerned about healthy living also tend to be interested in developing a more overtly spiritual attitude to life. In this chapter, therefore, the focus will mostly be on the discipline and enthusiasm parts of the spectrum, though we will return to the question of spirituality and everyday lifestyles in the final chapter.

Both discipline and enthusiasm are characteristic of traditional religious faiths, including Christianity of course, and until relatively recently they have tended to be the dominant concerns of the New Spirituality scene. Having loosened what they regarded as the shackles of a predetermined way of being, the leaders of the 1960s' cultural revolution were always looking for new experiences as well as new disciplines that would address their questions of personal identity and meaning, and because of the cultural matrix in which that revolution took place there was a natural predisposition to look almost anywhere except the Christian tradition. The kids of the sixties (of whom I am one) were literally like children in a toy shop, trying out anything and everything just because it was there. In that atmosphere it was inevitable that the spiritual concerns that both dominated and defined the early development of what was then called the 'New Age' would be non-mainstream and unorthodox. For a variety of reasons, it is this part of the spiritual spectrum that has attracted most attention from Christians, largely because alternative world views and non-Christian practices appeared to be in direct competition not only with the Church but also with those concepts of civil society that had historic connections with Christendom. With the benefit of hindsight, we can now see that the Churches had good reason to be concerned, because the people who became most interested in such alternatives were precisely those who already had a predisposition toward being interested in intentional spiritual practice, and whose interest had largely been sparked by their previous involvement with church life. The same trend can be discerned today, except that now (certainly in Europe, but increasingly in the USA) three or four generations have passed since such individuals had direct personal contact with the Christian faith. But it is still the case that the people most likely to be attracted to an intentional engagement with New Spirituality are the sort of people who in the past formed the natural constituency of the churches.[1] They probably have a memory of church life playing a central role in the lives of their parents or grandparents, and maybe even a sense of regret that what worked spiritually for previous generations no longer has the power to touch their own lives in meaningful ways. They are, however, still fired with the same sense of enthusiasm and purpose, and are prepared to make a serious commitment to making a difference to the wider society in which they live (now often defined in global rather than local terms) – but it is more likely to be through single-issue pressure groups than through the church.[2] For all these reasons, the attitudes that Christians adopt toward the spiritual concerns of such individuals is therefore more than just a matter of abstract theorizing, and will have a direct bearing on how – if at all – these people might in the future relate to the church and to Christian belief. It is not difficult to trace a variety of different Christian responses to this aspect of New Spirituality as it has evolved over the past thirty years or more, and in the first instance it will be worth reminding ourselves of what these are. I want to go much further than that, however, to suggest that a missiological engagement with New Spirituality requires us to unlearn much that has been taken for granted hitherto, and that taking this missiological imperative seriously requires us to redefine the terms in which we reflect theologically on what New Spirituality is all about.

Christians and the New Spirituality

Christian understandings of culture and of other world faiths have been well documented, and to a large extent a similar, if not identical, diversity of approaches can be traced with regard to New Spirituality. Traditional categories such as exclusivism, inclusivism, and pluralism are all easy to locate. There is, though, one obvious difference: whereas all Christians recognize the importance of having a reasoned approach to culture or to other world faiths, a significant number within the Churches appear to adopt a head-in-the-sand attitude to New Spirituality, and are in denial about the whole phenomenon. Yet the truth is that this is both the biggest single challenge and the most significant opportunity facing Christians in the West today – far more significant, in my opinion, than the so-called threat from Islam about which many Christians have become so paranoid.

How then do those Christians who think about it at all regard New Spirituality? Some have been more open than others by either embracing New Spirituality, or in some way incorporating insights from other spiritual traditions or disciplines into their own beliefs and practices. The most high-profile individual internationally here is probably Matthew Fox, who was first silenced by the Vatican and then subsequently thrown out of the Dominican Order precisely because he was deemed to have been too open to influences and understandings coming from the spirituality of this wider culture.[3] Fox certainly leaves himself open to critical scrutiny on a number of levels, but in my opinion he is nothing like as dangerous a person as he can be made out to be. Perhaps he is unwise in some of the things he has said and written, and he is certainly careless in relation to the way he tends to reimagine Christian history so that all the good guys look like Matthew Fox and all the bad guys look like Augustine (to whose influence he traces all the ills of the Christian tradition). But it is significant that not only did he accept the discipline of silence imposed on him by the Vatican, but when he was no longer welcome in the Roman Catholic Church, he chose not to abandon Christian belief but identified himself with another mainstream Christian tradition (Anglican). The reality is that many of his questions are absolutely on target in relation to the issues raised by the New Spirituality, matters related to global concerns such as the environment as well as personal empowerment and the misuse of theological categories such as sin to become instruments of social control and, inevitably it seems, exploitation.[4] But Matthew Fox is not the only one to have embraced New Spirituality. In the UK, there is the phenomenon which Darren Kemp has eloquently described as 'The Christaquarians'.[5] Among the leading lights in this movement, he lists Donald Reeves, rector of St James's (Church of England) Piccadilly (London) throughout the 1990s, who attracted attention to himself when he facilitated the establishment of a network called *Alternatives* which embraced a very eclectic collection of spiritual pathways and practices. As he explained in his strategic plan for the church, Donald Reeves never regarded *Alternatives* as a Christian group, but quite specifically saw it as a part of the church's evangelistic outreach that would at least place Christianity on the agenda of today's spiritual searchers, and present the church as a user-friendly institution. Other ventures that Kemp identifies as 'Christaquarian' include the work of Canon Peter Spink and the Omega Order, The Bridge Trust (Janice Dolley), Sophia (Kevin Tingay), the Grail Retreat Centre, Christian TM, The More-to-Life movement, and the network for Creation Centred Spirituality – these last four all associated with the name of Fr Adrian Smith, among others.

Some have regarded such initiatives as cutting-edge forms of evangelism, while others criticize them as being too ready to provide a platform for non-Christian spiritualities, and in the process abandoning central elements of the Christian tradition. It is probably the case that this negative view has been the dominant one. Unfortunately, the criticisms are not always well founded, not least because of the generally elementary understanding of the nature of New Spirituality that is exhibited by most Christians. Given that, it is probably inevitable that anyone who engages with it in any form at all will find themselves to be the target of criticisms and complaints. I have received enough complaints myself over the years, not for doing anything outrageously unChristian, but merely because I talk to people outside the church, and take their spiritual concerns seriously. I do not propose to engage more extensively with that particular discussion here, partly because those who have proactively incorporated insights from New Spirituality into their Christian praxis are in no sense representative of the attitude of the majority of Christians – but also because I believe there is a much bigger challenge to be faced here than merely scoring points against other opinions, whatever they may be.

Not all Christians are in denial about the challenge of New Spirituality. Indeed, there are some who seem to think about nothing else and talk more about New Spirituality than they do of God. In this group, the default position tends to be overwhelmingly negative, even aggressive, with talk about fighting battles to marginalize the influence of New Spirituality, and some even see themselves as caught up in the last great battle of Armageddon, struggling to push back the tide of a movement that they not only dislike, but believe to be the very embodiment of evil.[6]

Many strands have come together to engender this sort of attitude. One of them has nothing at all to do with theology or spirituality, but is simply a product of the essentially traditional preferences of very many Christian people. There are exceptions, of course, but generally speaking Christians do tend to be cautious, conservative people who dislike change and innovation of any kind. Many of them were as resistant to buying a television set in the 1950s as they would have been about going to a Reiki healer or an angel channeler in the 1990s. Though it is easy to adorn such suspicion with biblical texts and what look like theological principles, the major influence here is more likely to be personality type and habit rather than commitment to either gospel or church.[7] For people who are already insecure in a fast-changing world, rejection of New Spirituality is one way of maintaining a sense of personal safety: it preserves strong boundaries so we know who is 'in' and who is 'out' (whatever our definitions of those words might be), and it also has a tendency to demonize those whom we perceive as being 'out' in such a way as to ensure there will never be any dialogue with them – which, of course, is the last thing many Christians want anyway, for why would you talk to people whom you regard as being so incorrigibly corrupt?

Not that most people of this sort would like to admit that their attitudes are based on personal fear. Instead, they tend to portray New Spirituality as being a monstrous threat to the very future of civilization itself. It has even been claimed that the widespread interest in spirituality is connected to an underground resurgence of the Nazi movement, and those who believe this kind of thing talk of arming themselves for a spiritual confrontation with the powers of darkness. Spiritual searchers are dismissed as being demonically inspired, and their activities are to be resisted by any means possible. In the process, provocative terminology is used to create an atmosphere of irrational phobia about groups such as Wiccans – identifying them with 'witchcraft' and even 'Satanism' (though it is a well-documented fact that so-called Satanists are almost always atheists, believing in neither God nor Devil!).[8] As part of the creation of this atmosphere of paranoia, stories claiming to be personal testimonies have been circulated, allegedly documenting lurid practices such as child sacrifice, abduction by aliens, and so on. Of course, Christians are not the only ones who do this, and movies and TV programmes often present similar images.[9] But Christians, of all people, should have a longer memory. Anabaptists were subjected to the same sort of criticisms in the sixteenth century, and more recently in the early days of the charismatic movement the same sort of lurid claims and counter-claims were bandied about – while the history of Roman Catholicism and Protestantism is littered with conspiracy theories (from both sides).

Getting the facts right

But is any of this a reasonable understanding of the phenomenon of New Spirituality? In an essay published in 1992 surveying books written by evangelical Christians on what was then called the 'New Age', religion professor Irving Hexham concluded that Christians had no idea what they were talking about. Their works, he complained, are written 'in a simplistic style . . . characterized by reductionism, lack of definition, and poor scholarship'. Even worse, he alleged that some either 'deliberately distort their evidence or do not know how to read a text.'[10] That was a particularly damning criticism from a scholar who identified himself as being an evangelical Christian. The sort of books he was criticizing are still being written, but there has also been a noticeable – albeit gradual – shift of emphasis, as Christians have begun to appreciate that demonizing people in this way is merely reinforcing all the negative stereotypes that so many people already have of the Church and its members as being narrow-minded, bigoted, and judgemental. It may well be that the reason for this shift in attitude is more pragmatic than theological, but the ideas presented in a recent volume of which Prof. Hexham was himself one of the editors, and which is subtitled 'a holistic evangelical approach', are radically different from those represented by the sort of literature he criticized ten years before.[11] It is still the case, however, that many ordinary Christians – as opposed to those who have made a special study of this topic – live with the old attitudes. So it will be worthwhile, however briefly, to reflect on why Christians have evidently found it so difficult to connect with the burgeoning popular spirituality of our generation.

Philip Johnson is an Australian theologian who has spent many years both meeting and living with people who are intentionally engaged with the practices and disciplines of New Spirituality, and his experience points him in the same direction as Hexham's. He dismisses the validity of these negative attitudes to New Spirituality because he believes they derive from 'poor documentation, factual errors, and illogical arguments . . . they present unsubstantiated testimonies of people who claim they were witches . . . Christians take these stories too seriously'.[12] Fellow Australian Ross Clifford – lawyer, theologian, and principal of Morling College (Baptist Theological College of NSW) – concurs with this judgement, and argues that such negative approaches are actually preventing creative engagement with what he regards as a major mission opportunity in Western culture:

> The glut of books and seminars teaching negative or defensive apologetics toward New Spirituality has helped to create an evangelical climate of fear. New Spirituality is now viewed as a movement one apologetically holds the cross up to in order to protect the church and our children, rather

> than being a cultural group to which one takes the cross in order to evangelize.[13]

In a world where tabloid journalism is dominated by salacious muck-raking, I suppose we ought not to be surprised at the emergence of tabloid theology. Christians are often more conformed to the spirit of the age than they would care to admit. But my Australian colleagues are right, and by way of explaining why I think they are I want to draw attention to a number of significant considerations – some cultural, some theological, some biblical, but all of them have a significant bearing on the future of effective Christian witness and ministry in this area.

First of all, I want to reinforce what has already been said: that most Christians know next to nothing at all about New Spirituality, at any point on the spiritual spectrum outlined in the last chapter. This comes out repeatedly in many of the books and seminars that allegedly deal with it, for they all tend to recycle the same half-truths and untruths rather than deal with first-hand evidence. For example, it seems to be widely imagined among Christians that New Spirituality is a single monolithic entity of some kind – an impression that, admittedly, can be given by people like me using an actual term such as 'new spirituality' to describe it. Christians understand institutions and organizations – that is what the Church is, and has been since at least the period of Christendom – and they assume that anything that is culturally significant is also likely to have organizational consistency and some sort of central governing body, whose programme is determined by a set of core beliefs. On this assumption, it is widely claimed that today's spiritual searchers have a monistic world view, in which all things are not only interconnected, but also infused with some kind of spiritual, if not divine power. But this is simply not the case, and one does not need to look very far at all to find quite extremely dualistic world views being held in New Spirituality circles.[14] The present enthusiasm for angels would be a good example: you cannot believe in angels and be a monist. It just doesn't work like that.

In addition, however, Christians should also appreciate that to some extent the apparent success and growth of intentional involvement in New Spirituality has come about because the

Church has not taken it seriously and has had no effective engagement with it. By being absent from this expanding spiritual marketplace, the impression is given that Christian faith has no connection with the lifestyle issues that compel people to search for identity and meaning in the first place. If that is the impression that is being created, is it any wonder that spiritually serious people dismiss Christianity as being irrelevant, and explore those things that are actually accessible to them? Even if they don't fully satisfy, at least the offerings of New Spirituality are affirming the seriousness of their search, merely by being there. Of course, there is an extensive agenda behind the reluctance of Christians to connect with New Spirituality, and once again a sense of our own history can be illuminating in this respect. A hundred years ago, Christians gave the appearance of resisting the prognosis for the future of belief offered by the likes of Nietzsche, and argued against it in a disconnected philosophical way. But in the end, they accepted pragmatically what they assumed was the inevitability of his opinion and concluded that – while he was probably an extremist – belief in anything transcendent was, at best, going to face hard times, and the way to counteract that would be to co-opt the same kind of rationalist philosophical and historical-literary discourse in the service of reimagining Christian belief. Christian thinkers as radically different from one another as Rudolf Bultmann and his disciples at one end of the spectrum,[15] and evangelical Christians like T.C. Hammond and his followers at the other,[16] no doubt used quite different language to articulate their understandings and strategies, but at heart they were united in agreeing on where the threat was coming from. It was a rational challenge, and for that reason would need to be tackled by analytical, propositional argumentation based on an essentially Cartesian view of the world and of human nature. I have often wondered whether these people were deliberately perverse in choosing to argue about matters such as 'demythologizing' Christian faith at the very same time as Einstein was promoting his revolutionary ideas that would within a couple of generations 'remythologize' not just scientific theory, but our entire world view. Or was it that they were so out of touch with the wider culture, that it just never occurred to them to make the connection? Whatever the answer to that question, the outcome was that by the 1960s the Church ended up arguing about things like the death of God,[17] while popular culture had moved in entirely different directions and was hailing celebrities who not only took God's existence for granted, but were prepared to travel around the world in search of spiritual meaning because it seemed as if traditional belief systems no longer connected with anything anyone wanted to know about. At the time, it was Mircea Eliade (a historian of religion) who almost alone challenged the theological consensus. Drawing attention to the universality of belief in what he called 'sky and sky gods' (i.e. a supernaturalistic and transcendent world view), he proposed that the entire *Death of God* debate was founded on a mistaken understanding of God that attempted to define God in neat rational categories and in the process lost a sense of the mystery of ultimate being.[18] A major contributing factor to this misreading of the culture by theologians must be the inherited predilection of the discipline to pay attention to high culture and to regard popular culture as inconsequential and irrelevant to the development of a significant world view. During the month when I was delivering the lectures on which this book is based, I often wondered what the audiences for the first series of London Lectures in the 1970s would have thought had they known that New Spirituality would now be considered worthy of serious investigation. It was in that same decade that I completed a Ph.D. on Gnosticism, and most of my Christian friends thought that by doing so I had allowed myself to be diverted from what they would have regarded as topics of more obvious relevance to the mission and ministry of the Church. But reading the signs of the times – and being ahead of the game in doing so – is one of the fundamental callings of Christian leadership. And knowing which signs to be reading is absolutely crucial.[19] While I am encouraged by the increasing seriousness with which Christians are beginning to engage with the concerns of the New Spirituality, I fear that it may be too little and too late, for the reality is that we should now be looking ahead to discern the trends of the future as the world becomes an ever more uncertain place.

A third question to be considered in articulating an appropriate Christian engagement with New Spirituality is a very simple one that invites some self-reflection, namely what do we think we are doing? Or, if you prefer, what do we think we ought to be doing? What are Christians for, and why is the Church here at all? One of the key documents of the Second Vatican Council was introduced by this statement: 'The pilgrim church is missionary by her very nature'.[20] At this point in time, the importance of that priority can hardly be over-emphasized. The overall decline in Christian practice in the Western world is such that, unless the Church is indeed missionary, it faces a very uncertain future – according to some, no future at all. I assume that those who are left in the churches are bothered about this. They ought to be, and if they are not, I find it hard to understand why they would still be there at all. The extent of any individual's personal spirituality can be gauged by the level of enthusiasm with which they want to share their story with other people. Yet until very recently, there has been no serious effort at a missionary engagement with New Spirituality, and even today the prevailing approach is certainly not missionary. So why is it that in a generation that has given so much thought to how the gospel might be shared effectively in even the remotest corners of the earth there is so little appreciation of the missionary opportunity and challenge presented by the rise of New Spirituality?

Here again, lethargy and disinterest in the facts of history are a major part of the answer. I still meet Christians who, though they might accept the demise of Christendom in a theoretical sort of way, still behave as if it was intact.[21] Instead of recognizing Western society as a mission field in which the gospel needs to be contextualized, they assume that being Western and Christian are coterminous, and that Christian witness is about recalling people to a faith they still hold, albeit in some attenuated form. This attitude manifests itself through the growth of increasingly vociferous pressure groups who complain to the media about the infringement of Christian values – as if these values are self-evident to the wider culture. But why would anyone expect a post-Christian (and now post-secular) society to espouse Christian values? No one would ever dream of complaining that an Islamic culture was not Christian, so by what logic do we have the right to complain about Western society for not being Christian? Admittedly, the picture is somewhat clouded by the numbers of people who said in the 2001 UK census that they identified with being 'Christian', though as we saw in an earlier chapter the meaning of that is open to various interpretations. But in view of the vast disparity between the numbers who exhibit some sympathy for being 'Christian' and those who actually connect with the church, the best that can be said is that a lot of people admire what they know of Jesus, but have little confidence in what they see in the life of the churches.

Inherited attitudes

Why are Christians apparently so afraid of meaningful engagement with spiritual searchers, regarding such individuals as people whose views are to be refuted, condemned, and argued against, rather than redeemed? At least three factors seem to be operating here. The most obvious is that spiritual searchers can actually be quite threatening, though not in the sense that Christians sometimes imagine them to be. In my experience, people who are intentionally searching for spiritual meaning have no inhibitions or reservations in sharing their personal story. They speak openly and easily about what they have found to be true, and how it impacts their life, and they also tend to speak with equal frankness about the things they still struggle with. For many Christians, this level of honesty is both embarrassing and intimidating, for it invites reciprocal reflection on our own personal pilgrimage and creates a space in which there is an expectation that we will share our own innermost experiences. All too often this leaves Christian people with little or nothing to say. We know how to talk in abstractions about doctrine or belief systems, but we do not speak with the same ease about personal experience of the spiritual, and in some cases the depth of questioning that others reveal in themselves can serve to expose the shallowness with which Christians on occasion approach their own faith. Related to this is a spiritual paranoia among many Christians who display an unhealthy obsession with the activities of what they perceive to be demons, accompanied by a corresponding lack of confidence in God. I find it very hard to understand why Christians should be so impressed by the power of evil: not only is it disempowering in terms of mission, but it is also, in the final analysis, heretical in relation to orthodox Christian belief. I will return to this later in the chapter. For now, we need to consider a third factor that seems to inhibit missiological engagement with New Spirituality, and this emerges from the unthinking adoption of sloppy definitions of the phenomenon as a whole. For example, rather than the term 'New Spirituality' (or even 'New Age'), one often hears talk of 'alternative spirituality'. That immediately raises the further question, 'alternative to what?' When Christians start thinking like that, it is only natural to conclude 'alternative to the gospel' – an understanding which has a tendency to engender two further erroneous assumptions. One is that New Spirituality is in competition with the gospel in the sense of being actively involved in promoting itself as anti-Christian and anti-gospel. While there are exceptions to every rule, the reality is that the vast majority of people engaged on an intentional spiritual search today have such scant knowledge of the gospel that it would never occur to them to be either for or against it. It simply does not register on their scale of spiritual possibilities. The other assumption that Christians tend to make is the most damaging of all in terms of effective mission, namely the idea that New Spirituality is a perverted form of the Christian message. This particular assumption runs very deep. Some of the early Christian writers on the topic undoubtedly created that impression,[22] but even today if you go to a Christian bookstore to find books on this subject you will most likely find them in a section labelled 'cults' or some similar terminology. In a sociological sense, very little of what goes on in New Spirituality could be described as a cult. But neither could it be described as a cult in theological terms, where that word tends to invoke quite specific images, predominantly of a group of new religious movements of the nineteenth century, which did indeed derive from Judeo-Christian roots, and therefore could with some justification be regarded as corrupted forms of the gospel. In this category would be movements such as Jehovah's Witnesses, the Church of Jesus Christ of Latter-Day Saints (Mormons), Christian Science, and a cluster of smaller groups. Christians think they know how to deal with such people: they denounce them, they pray against them, and when they get the chance they argue with them about detailed points of biblical interpretation. It is not difficult to see where this confrontational way of dealing with ideas that are perceived as heresy came from. Its roots are to be found in Christendom, when every deviant Western world view was indeed a variation on mainstream Christianity, and the Church saw its responsibility as being to recall such people to a faith that they had once held in its purity. These people were not non-Christians, needing to be evangelized, but wayward Christians who needed to be called to account and corrected – and, if they refused to fall into line, to be condemned. In reality, there is little evidence that this approach ever actually worked, and groups like those mentioned continue to thrive (especially Mormonism) and converts from any of them to the Church are few and far between. What I am describing here as New Spirituality, however, is in no sense a deviant form of Christian belief, and to think of it as a cult (either sociologically or theologically) is quite inappropriate. It is more like the equivalent of a different world faith, though that parallel needs immediate qualification because there are at least four significant differences:

- Whereas world faiths in the traditional mode have a distinctive world view that gives coherence to everything else, there is no single coherent world view at all that can be identified as 'New Spirituality'. There is nothing to join, no headquarters, no single dominant vision. It is, in the words of Elliot Miller, a 'metanetwork', 'a network of networks'.[23]
- Partly related to that, New Spirituality is more of an internal phenomenon than an external one. It is essentially a personal pathway, whether individuals construct their own spiritual practices or adopt patterns that are more widely accepted and promoted.
- In line with this, the overwhelming emphasis is on personal practice, and not on dogma or belief. People can – and do – adopt practices without any reference at all to any original underlying ideology there may ever have been. Pragmatism is central: whatever 'works' is the touchstone of what is 'true' (though in the process, both words are redefined somewhat, which is why I place them in quotes here).
- Within this frame of reference, New Spirituality is highly

> eclectic. It cannot justly be criticized for not being Christian, because it might well incorporate elements of Christian belief and practice that are perfectly mainstream and orthodox.

For all these reasons, it seems to me that the central theological core of New Spirituality is not rooted in ideas or beliefs, but in people. Taking that further, I would propose that the most useful existing category with which to reflect on it is to see spiritual searchers as a distinct 'people group'. Not everyone is in this people group,[24] but it is sufficiently large and influential to demand serious attention by the Church. It is, quite literally, a different culture, with its own language, its own conventions, its own expectations and forms of life: an *unreached* people group, to use missiological jargon.

A traditional Chinese proverb expresses very concisely what might be involved in reaching a people group:

> Go to the people, Live among them, Learn from them, Love them. Start with what they know, Build on what they have.

To reach a people group requires understanding of the culture of that group, a willingness to address cultural barriers that prevent or inhibit people from 'hearing the gospel', and a creative approach to building relevant cultural bridges that might facilitate communication of the Christian message in such a way that it can be received as what it claims to be, namely 'good news'. It requires us to 'understand not only what [other people] believe, but also sympathetically understand why they do the things they do' and on that basis 'to proclaim the gospel in ways that are heard and understood, not ways that are rejected because they are not heard clearly and are therefore misunderstood.'[25] To contextualize the gospel effectively in the culture that is New Spirituality will require a radical about-turn on the part of most Christians, and the adoption of a completely different approach: not the 'formulaic evangelism based on a Christendom model', but 'a biblically informed approach to cross-cultural mission'.[26] Of course, behind that statement is the assumption that Christians ought to be engaging with New Spirituality in order to evangelize – an assumption that is by no means universally shared especially among evangelical Christians, who have generally been much more interested in refutation and in what John Morehouse eloquently describes as 'worldview annihilation' (and who in their right minds would line up to be annihilated?).[27]

Mission and New Spirituality

For those who see New Spirituality as a mission field rather than a battlefield, there is plenty of inspiration in the Christian tradition. In recent years there has been a good deal of discussion about the importance of Christians being 'incarnational', a term that has typically been used to describe the sort of thing that is recommended in the Sermon on the Mount where Jesus speaks of disciples being salt and light within the wider society of which they are a part (Matthew 5:13-16). But the notion of such incarnational ministry has tended to be embraced more eagerly in relation to matters of social concern than in relation to aspects of mission that connect more specifically with Christian theology. Even as I write it, I realize that is a somewhat clumsy way of putting it, because I would want to see both these aspects of Christian life and witness as intrinsically connected. Indeed, I would say that mission is not authentically Christian unless they are. But what I mean is that while there has been a tendency for Christians to be relatively caring and compassionate in addressing issues such as social deprivation, they have also tended to be aggressive and confrontational when speaking more overtly of faith. It is not difficult to understand the reasons for this. The cultural context of Western life for the last five hundred years or so has prioritized and valued the rational over the experiential. As a consequence, Christian beliefs have been presented in the form of propositional statements or truth claims in a more or less disembodied way. Journeying with another person as he or she tackles the existential challenges of everyday life cannot be done without personal engagement and empathy, whereas talking about belief systems in abstractions neither necessitates nor encourages an atmosphere of mutual engagement on a personal level. By definition, propositional forms of communication tend to set up conflict ('If I am right, you must be wrong'). They are a polarizing influence. Some would say that this kind of conflict is actually what the gospel is about, because it is always going to involve challenge to change, and for that reason not everyone will like it and respond in positive ways. But the problem is that all too often, aggressive disembodied forms of so-called evangelism do not lead to conflicts about the gospel, but arguments about human relationships, about control, exploitation and personal attitudes – and in the midst of all that, the actual challenge of the gospel itself is never heard. It is widely recognized that when those who report the news become the news themselves, something has gone seriously wrong. The same is true of Christian witness: if those who are called to bear witness themselves become the topic of conversation, then the essential message is displaced by the medium of communication. Of course, it should never be forgotten that the medium is the message, so if the negative attitudes of the messengers take centre stage a message is indeed being communicated: something like, 'If you too want to be angry, narrow-minded, repressed, etc., then join the church'. I hope it does not need to be said that this is not the gospel!

If an exclusively propositional approach to evangelism can encourage Christians to adopt confrontational attitudes, it can also have a dehumanizing effect on others who may be spiritually searching. Nobody wants to be told they are wrong, and it is a perfectly natural human response to become defensive when that happens. Anyone who has ever had a doorstep conversation with Jehovah's Witnesses will know what I am talking about, because they have honed this form of confrontational witness into an art form. This is where we can reconnect with comments that were made in the previous chapter regarding the importance of the story as a significant key to positive Christian engagement with New Spirituality. For a story does not evoke confrontation in the same way as propositions. When I share the story of my spiritual journey, I am not tempted to insist that others should replicate it, because I know they are not me and the detailed circumstances of their lives will be quite different from my own. But for all the same reasons, those who hear the story of my personal faith journey are unlikely to argue about it or disagree with it, because you cannot do that with another person's story. You may have questions about it, and some aspects may sound odd, or even hard to believe. But you cannot tell me it is wrong because, for all its uniqueness, it is my story. The same thing is true if we faithfully tell the story of Jesus – the story, that is, rather than the 'meaning' of the story. Those with whom we engage will be far more likely to reflect again on a story than they will be on ideas expressed in abstractions. Propositions invite you to take sides, to be for or against; stories invite you to become part of them, to compare and contrast other stories with your own story, and from that starting point to reflect and wonder about the meaning of it all. To connect effectively with spiritual searchers, Christians need to rediscover the power of story – their own stories, other people's stories, and God's story – and understand that it is in this three-way relational matrix that the gospel is likely to be most truly heard, and acted upon.

In reality, of course, this style of relational witness has attracted a good deal of attention among church folk in recent years. The theory behind the best-selling Alpha course is based on something like this, though its delivery in local settings easily and often degenerates into confrontation. There are plenty of reasons why attention has been focused in this direction, not least of which must be the singular failure of those disembodied propositional forms of witness that have prevailed in recent times. If this aggressive approach was not actually the cause of church decline in Western culture, it has certainly done nothing to reverse it. But the point I want to make here is that in relation to mission with people who are attracted to the disciplines and practices of New Spirituality, there has been little evidence of this relational style, and the confrontational approach has prevailed, typically by regarding them as dangerous and demon possessed and therefore to be fought against and resisted.

Various models from Christian history have been identified in the effort to discern a way forward that will both be relevant to today's culture while also being rooted in the tradition. Two of these are worth further reflection here: Celtic spirituality, and even long before that, the biblical example of St Paul in Athens. Both of these have the advantage that they are forms of Christian witness located in a predominantly non-Christian culture, but a culture in which spirituality (by various definitions) was evidently high on the agenda.

Models from history

When it comes to ancient Celtic spirituality, there has been no shortage of sceptics who will tell us that we have insufficient certain knowledge about this period of history to be able to say anything useful about it, and they complain that the way it is being talked about today is incompatible with serious historical research.[28] It is certainly true that at some points the evidence is very sketchy, and some claims made about the ancient Celts are based on a romanticized image rather than hard facts that can be established beyond reasonable doubt. But it is equally true that the Judeo-Christian tradition has always taken images from past history – however shadowy – and reinterpreted and reapplied them for the needs of a new day. One might argue that the Old Testament prophets spent much of their time doing just that, as they constantly looked back to the formative events of their nation's life (the exodus and the giving of the Law in particular), and used these dimly remembered episodes as a basis on which to challenge and encourage people who were living in quite different social circumstances. The New Testament evangelists also regarded the stories of Jesus in the same light, and reinterpreted and applied them to different situations and circumstances that went well beyond their original location in first-century Palestine. In reality, the distinction that has been made between so-called 'Celtic' and 'Roman' styles scarcely depends on a deep cultural understanding of either of these historic entities, and the way in which recent writers have used such terms does not demand a direct connection with either Celts or Romans.[29] It is a convenient terminology for talking of two different ways of doing things, with 'Celtic' being relational or incarnational, and 'Roman' being propositional, analytic and detached. If it helps people to think that this is not an altogether new struggle in the history of the Church, then all well and good. But it would be just as possible to use entirely different language to characterize it: 'male' (=Roman) and 'female' (=Celtic) spring to mind as suitable alternatives, though again without needing to imply that all men will behave in one way and all women in the other. It would be just as accurate to describe the same distinction in terms of the dichotomy between biblical values and the attitudes typified by Christendom.

On this taxonomy, the 'Celtic' model lays emphasis on

- the integrity of the messenger ('the medium is the message')
- the content of the message expressed holistically through story, symbol, music, ritual, and so on
- the message connecting with everyday life and the concerns of ordinary people
- the importance of community: mission teams, monastic communities, and shared responsibility. These features at least are well documented in ancient Celtic Christianity
- a recognition that God is at work in this world in many different ways, and therefore all life is sacred, and can be redeemed
- 'belonging before believing'
- theologically, an emphasis on blessing: God is more likely to be portrayed as joyful and playful rather than angry and resentful.

The 'Roman' model more or less reflects the opposite of these things, in particular:

- a dualism that allows the messenger to be disconnected from 'the message'
- an exclusive emphasis on the message as cognitive, propositional, rational – and certainly suspicious of any other way of accessing reality, if not overtly condemnatory of anything to do with human imagination
- an emphasis on individualism rather than community
- a rigid distinction between the sacred and the secular, with a consequent differentiation between the concerns of church and the needs of everyday life
- a strong control mechanism that insists on 'belief' before 'belonging'
- theologically, an emphasis on sinning, and the portrayal of God as primarily angry and vengeful.

Whether you call them 'Celtic' and 'Roman' or something else, the reality highlighted by these different ways of thinking cannot be denied. In point of fact, the tension between these two modes of being and believing can be traced right back to the lifetime of Jesus himself, who generally exemplified this 'Celtic' model, sometimes to the dismay of his disciples who would have been much happier with a different approach (Mark 9:38-41, Luke 9:52-5). Paradoxically, some of them would never have got to be disciples in the first place had Jesus insisted on the 'Roman' approach! In an article written some considerable time ago, I argued that Paul also displays the same traits as Jesus in this regard,[30] and it is to his example that I now wish to turn in the search for another, complementary missiological angle on the New Spirituality.

A biblical model

The particular episode in question here is the story in Acts 17:16-34 where we find the account of Paul's encounter with the pluralistic culture of ancient Athens. There is a remarkable similarity between this and the context in which we live and minister today. Though the term was never used in the ancient world, Athens was the quintessential 'supermarket of faiths'. Moreover, the cultural reasons for this bear an uncanny resemblance to those trends which we have already documented in recent Western history. Centuries before the time of Paul, the philosophers of ancient Greece had questioned the usefulness of the inherited traditional spirituality of their culture. Ordinary people had a feeling that the things that inspired their forebears no longer made sense – but for the most part, they found that those who deconstructed the traditions failed to offer any meaningful alternatives. The sceptics might be right, but their ideas were largely inaccessible to all but an educated élite, and for most people their teachings appeared arid and meaningless as a foundation for everyday life. As a result, a spiritual vacuum was created, into which came flooding all manner of esoteric spiritual beliefs and practices from other times and places, and out of which eventually emerged that mish-mash of mythology and speculative psychology that came to be known as Gnosticism –

and which has more than a passing resemblance to much of the intentionally disciplined aspects of the New Spirituality scene today.[31]

Given all these similarities between Paul's circumstances and our own, we can do worse than ask ourselves what we might learn from the paradigm of mission set out by Luke in the way this story is told. At the same time, we need to be aware of the differences between the first century and our own situation. A major difference is to be found in the fact that for first-century people a significant part of the appeal of Christianity was that it itself was a 'new spirituality'. That fact alone undoubtedly gave the apostles an easier challenge than the one we face in a post-Christian society, where Christianity is generally viewed through the somewhat negative spectacles of the cultural and historical baggage of Crusades, Inquisition, Colonialism, and those other life-denying episodes from the world of Christendom which we surveyed in the first chapter.

Having said this, there are at least three obvious points of connection between St Paul's evangelistic praxis as reported in this story and what I am advocating in relation to Christian engagement with today's New Spirituality:[32]

There is a need to listen before we speak. There are two elements in this as Luke reports it. The first is that Paul spent time in the city of Athens, listening and observing, before he started to engage with people. Luke is very honest in the way he reports this, and implies that Paul was so uncomfortable with what he encountered that he could do little else, not least because his two companions had been left behind in Thessalonica, and he needed to await their arrival before he would have the courage to begin serious spiritual conversations in this alien environment. But whatever the reason for it, Paul started by immersing himself in the popular culture of the streets. He invested time in just being there, wandering round the city observing and listening, meeting with the people of the city.

In addition to that, however, he had certainly done his homework, and he knew enough about Athenian history and spirituality to be able to relate his message to it in relevant ways. Back in the sixth century BC Epimenides, the Cretan hero and philosopher, had been called to Athens to help the city to overcome a terrible plague. The Athenians' own oracle had declared that the city was under a curse because of war crimes committed in the past, and none of the deities they worshipped seemed to have the power to lift the curse. As a way of resolving this dilemma, Epimenides proposed that there may be a deity whose name they did not yet know. To test this hypothesis, he sent some sheep out onto Mars Hill to graze and decreed that if any sheep lay down they would be sacrificed on an altar dedicated to this unknown god. Some did lay down, and they were sacrificed – and the plague was duly lifted. It can hardly be coincidence that the story in Acts 17:16-34 not only refers to such an altar, but also quotes from Epimenides.

It would be interesting to know which particular way of listening to the culture of Athens was the more challenging to Paul: what he heard on the streets, or what he learned in the academy. This highlights a major question for us today in relation to mission in the context of New Spirituality – to whom do we listen, and how do we listen? By history and habit, Christians have a predisposition to listen to the ideologues of high culture. In the past, that certainly gave access to social and intellectual trendsetters, but following the same pathway today can actually distance us from the cultural challenges with which the Church should be engaging. Until relatively recently, it was indeed the case that high culture was the driving force that determined the belief systems of ordinary people. The intellectual classes were also the chattering classes, whose opinions gradually filtered down to impact the attitudes of the wider population. But today, popular opinion is formulated not from the top downwards, but from the bottom upwards. People no longer trust those who are supposed to be 'somebody', whether they be politicians, business people, academics – or the Church. The growth of the mass media has made it possible for us all to know a good deal more than previous generations did about those who are at the head of our institutions – and we can see that, far from having some specially privileged insights, they are actually struggling with the same things as everyone else. Moreover, the worldwide web has given a voice to millions of ordinary people whose opinions would have been unheard in the past, but who can now post their ideas on their own blog sites and share them in chat rooms, and are finding that others empathize with them and take them seriously. No group that aspires to make a difference in contemporary society can afford to ignore that reality. Of course, the denizens of high culture need to hear the gospel just as much as others. But in accordance with my concern to maintain a clear missiological focus to this discussion, we should not lose sight of the fact that they are the very people who singularly failed to discern the emergence of New Spirituality as a significant force in the life of Western culture, and even today many of them dismiss it as the pathological ramblings of a civilization in decline rather than the potent force that it clearly is in the lives of very large numbers of people. This is the very same mentality that failed to recognize the long-term significance of what was going on in the 1960s, and whose influence at that time encouraged Christians to address the questions of a fading Cartesian rationality instead of engaging with the popular culture of people who followed the Beatles in a new search for transcendence, and who of course are now middle-aged leaders of business and culture – the very ones whose concern to find meaning and purpose in life has been a major catalyst in the growing popularity of New Spirituality.

Theologian Tex Sample regards this 'class captivity of the church' as a major hindrance to effective mission, and laments the way that theological discourse is so heavily dependent on high culture. He certainly does not mince words by describing it all as 'highly differentiated language used to comb the innards of the privileged' – something which can only serve to consolidate the 'rituals of supremacy' whose dominance he believes to be a significant factor in the accelerating decline of the Church throughout the West. Indeed, he goes further and suggests that our continued love affair with cultural élitism undermines what he regards as central themes of the gospel, by implying that other people's preferences are simplistic and inadequate and therefore those who make such choices will need to be controlled and improved by others who know better. In the process, he raises the obvious, but fundamental, missiological question: 'Who would want to join that kind of organization?'[33] These comments are absolutely on target in relation to the way many Christians have thought about the New Spirituality.

An effective connection with any people group must begin

with authentic understanding, taking seriously what we hear and treating all opinions and attitudes with the respect they deserve, because those holding them are women and men 'made in the image of God' (Genesis 1:26-7).

There is a call to journey with people. St Paul's starting point in Athens was the experienced spiritual journey of his hearers. To use language previously adopted in this book, his own story of faith was always shared in the context of the personal stories of other people. We can be pretty certain that this is an authentic account of Paul's regular practice, because it is not only emphasized by Luke (the author of Acts) but also in Paul's own writings (1 Corinthians 9:19-23). In many instances, Paul began in the synagogue with people who were readers of the Hebrew scriptures. It was natural for him to start there, because his own background was in Judaism. Until relatively recently, Christians in Western culture began from a roughly similar place, because almost everyone knew what was in the Bible, even if they rarely read it or took it very seriously. But it is only in a story like this account of his mission in Athens that the radical nature of Paul's practice becomes apparent. For the starting point here was a collection of things that, in his heart, Paul was uneasy about – not only the altar to an unknown god, but much more besides. In terms of mission within a context of New Spirituality, the most significant lesson to be drawn from this story is that he did not begin by dismissing these things, and telling the Athenians what they had got wrong. He did not enter the supermarket of faiths in order to empty the shelves. Nor did he criticize them, or dismiss or belittle their spiritual search – still less engage in 'spiritual warfare' by declaring them to be demon possessed, in the way that many Christians have done in relation to some aspects of New Spirituality, notably those that are to be found at the discipline or enthusiasm points on the spectrum. On the contrary, he affirmed what he found there, and accepted other people's concerns as valid starting points for the spiritual pilgrimage that is the Christian journey. Not only that, but throughout the entire account Luke makes not even the slightest suggestion that Paul used the Bible at all! He did of course share the story of Jesus, but it appears that St Paul was able to communicate a completely acceptable version of the gospel without once referring to the scriptures, while at the same time quoting from traditional Greek literature.

Developing a willingness to begin with the concerns of New Spirituality is possibly one of the biggest challenges for today's Christians. For this is a clear move away from the models associated with the past. Instead of expecting other people to be concerned with our interests, we will need to engage with theirs. For practical inspiration on how to do it, we will need to pay close attention to the evangelistic style not only of Paul but also of Jesus, for both of them exemplify this. And for theological grounding, we will need to revisit our beliefs on creation and incarnation, asking what we really do mean when we say that people – as human beings – are 'made in God's image' (Genesis 1:27). Since our traditional evangelistic endeavours have been based more on doctrines of fall and redemption, this will require a major paradigm shift. It is instructive that, in his magisterial account of mission through the ages, David Bosch was unable to find a single historical model of mission that began from a doctrine of creation.[34] Yet here in Paul's engagement with Athens, creation and our shared humanity is the starting point, as it always will be if our evangelism is to lead to the establishment of communities which will be effective outposts of God's kingdom.

This may not sound too challenging until we start to get specific in identifying the 'altars to unknown gods' in today's New Spirituality. For this is where the questions get more difficult for some in relation to journeying with others. In a previous chapter it was pointed out that some Christians have identified rather enthusiastically with what I called the lifestyle or more 'secular' end of the spiritual spectrum, characterized by a concern for 'living a good life'. But many Christians have no idea how to engage creatively with other parts of that spectrum. This is especially true of the part of the spectrum I have called 'discipline', and at the point where it connects with or runs into enthusiasm. Can things like divination, astrology, the Tarot, channeling, and the many distinctive therapies that are on offer here really provide openings for the gospel? One of my previous books is *Beyond Prediction*, which is subtitled *the Tarot and your Spirituality*. I wrote it in partnership with Ross Clifford and

Philip Johnson, who have already been mentioned in this chapter, and we intentionally addressed it not to Christians but to people whose 'unknown god' is the Tarot.[35] It was not written in a vacuum, but rather on the basis of extensive experience over a number of years of being a Christian presence in psychic fairs, mind, body and spirit festivals, and similar places. We knew that the Tarot was indeed one of today's most popular altars, and also that it could be used to introduce people to faith in Christ – not least because we know people who have actually come to faith through this route, some of whom have entered full-time Christian ministry. Moreover, before engaging in this ministry we did our homework to discover the origins of the Tarot cards, and the ways in which other people use them. All this and more is documented in the book, so there is no need to repeat it here. When the book was published, it produced two very opposite reactions from other Christians. On the one hand were those who acclaimed it as an innovative and truly incarnational form of evangelism for today's world. On the other were those who denounced it in the strongest possible terms, some even accusing us of being Satanically inspired. It was to be expected that Christians with a highly developed dualistic world view would not like it, because its underlying approach challenged the 'them and us' approach to contemporary spirituality. But among other groups, the last year or two has seen some remarkable endorsements of our approach and following the encouragement given not only by the book but by the many seminars the three of us have conducted both separately and together, Christians all over the world (including Britain) are now to be found with a positive presence in mind, body, spirit festivals – some of them using the Tarot, others offering something as simple as 'free prayer' – and people are coming to faith.[36]

I mention this not as an excuse for self-indulgent justification for any of this, but because it highlights the fact that recognizing and using the 'altars to unknown gods' as a platform for evangelism is likely to raise significant theological questions, of a sort that most Christians would rather avoid. The one key theological question which we had to deal with in relation to the Tarot was this: does the *missio Dei* have limits? Can God be found at work, at least potentially, absolutely everywhere? Or is God's activity limited in some way? Put simply, are there 'no-go' areas for God? And if there are, what does this imply about our view of who God is? In the light of the consistent practice of both Jesus and Paul – not to mention my underlying conviction about who I think God really is – it would be theological and spiritual suicide to embrace an understanding that would exclude God from any area of human life, no matter how alien it might seem, or how threatening to conventional Christian wisdom. Actually, the Tarot is by no means the only such 'altar' to be found in New Spirituality. Crystals, colours, healings, angels – all of these and more besides can become avenues for the invitation to follow Jesus. To identify these 'altars' we need to ask just one simple question in relation to any spiritual practice that we may find: does it focus attention on matters that are central to the gospel, even when the name of Christ is never mentioned? That was certainly one of the things that convinced me the Tarot could appropriately be used in this way, for its central images all originate from the Bible, and specifically from those aspects of the Bible that might be called archetypal, in the sense that they direct attention to key questions about meaning, purpose, and identity: who am I, why am I here, and how can I be the best person I can possibly be while I am here? More recently – and as if to underline what is said here – I was presented with a new pack of cards by someone who is a Tarot reader (and not a Christian). She introduced me to them with the recommendation that 'this is the most powerful set of cards I have ever come across'. Why was I not surprised when I saw what she had given me? The outside of the box identified them as 'The Jesus Deck', and the contents consist of four suits (like the Tarot, and regular playing cards) named after the four Gospels, Matthew, Mark, Luke and John. Each card has an illustration of a particular gospel story, together with a quotation from the relevant New Testament passage.

When people express surprise at my confidence that the Christian gospel can connect with even the most esoteric aspects of New Spirituality, my response (based on such experiences) is to wonder why we find it so difficult. When Philip the Evangelist encountered an Ethiopian who was searching for spiritual meaning, he asked him a fairly obvious question: 'Do you understand what you are reading?' (Acts 8:30). It so happened that he was reading the Hebrew scriptures, which Philip then explained to him. Today's spiritual searchers are not usually reading Christian books. But if we believe that this is God's world, and that God is at work in it, it seems obvious to me that God is likely to be lurking with missional intent in many of the things that people are reading and watching. We might feel more at ease talking about the Bible, but we are hardly likely to make sense to people if we ask them, 'Do you understand what you are not reading?' Yet my experience shows that when we engage with spiritual searchers in relation to the concerns they actually have, they are quite likely to want to know more about the source of Christian wisdom, and perhaps read the Bible for themselves. This is not rocket science: it is just common sense. Philip Johnson is right when he affirms that 'pagans are among the easiest people to convert'[37] – a claim for which there is ample evidence from church history as well as the experience of those who minister in this context today. But it raises the question of why the Church continues to expend so much time and energy in the effort of sharing the gospel with rationalist-materialists, who by definition will find it much harder to accept any connection with the transcendent, when spiritual searchers are already operating within the same frame of reference as biblical Christianity.

We need to be realistic about mission. The account of Paul in Athens also contains a cautionary warning. Christians, above all people, seem to desire results without much effort. There is a tendency to reduce Christian spirituality – including Christian mission – to the application of a formula which will deliver more or less immediate dividends, preferably in large quantities. By this measure, Paul's achievement in Athens can indeed be made to look insignificant. In truth, however, the New Testament offers us no reason to suppose that the presentation of the gospel will automatically lead to large numbers of converts. Jesus specifically said that discipleship would be tough, and Paul certainly knew that from his own experience (2 Corinthians 11:21-33). The only story in Acts that might challenge this is the account of the Day of Pentecost when 3000 were converted (Acts 2:1-41). But the entire point of that narrative is that those 3000 individuals were from all over the Jewish Diaspora. Three thousand people coming to faith in Jesus on that occasion did not result in a church of 3000 people in Jerusalem. On the contrary, all the evidence from the first century depicts the Jerusalem church as small and struggling – and many of the churches founded by Paul in Greece and Asia Minor fell into the same category. Mission in a context of New Spirituality will likewise be demanding, complex, challenging – and rewarding. Here, in particular, it is likely to be a matter of journeying with people over the medium- to long-term rather than an occasion for instant results. A mission mentality that replaces this biblical sense of spiritual process with a purely hedonistic sense of optimism will obscure some key features of Christian discipleship – in particular the central importance of the balance between the joyful and the painful, the comic and the tragic, which is endemic to all human life and spiritual growth. As today's spiritual searchers wrestle with the realities of life in the twenty-first century, the one thing they do know is that the cross needs to precede resurrection, if only because that is their lived experience – whether we are looking at lifestyles, discipline, or enthusiasm. To understand the relationship between life, death, rebirth and personal empowerment we need to revisit the power of the Christian story, and this is where we head in our final chapter.

4 Creating Churches for Spiritual Searchers

The words 'church' and 'spiritual searchers' do not sit easily together in the same sentence. There are many reasons why some Christians feel distinctly uncomfortable in relating to those who want to be 'spiritual' but not 'religious'. Some of them are directly related to the sort of misinformation and paranoia referred to in a previous chapter. But there are other factors at work here that are more obviously rooted in the experience of church life at local level. For the last fifteen years, I have been leading seminars and workshops in churches of all denominations and all around the world, and the one thing that strikes me over and over again is the extent to which Christians seem to lack any confidence in speaking about their own spiritual journey not only with people in the wider culture, but even with others in their own congregations. That may seem an odd comment coming so soon after I have suggested that some Christians are almost over-confident in a self-assured and aggressive way. But actually the two things might be manifestations of the same trend, for when we are uncertain of something that we also feel deeply about (in any sphere of life) there is a temptation to protect our opinions from external scrutiny while also shouting very loud in order to defend them. Politicians do it all the time: the weaker the argument, the more noise they make about it. It is a sad fact that many Christians do not know how to relate to others because they are insecure and uncertain about their own spirituality, and so they either resort to the sort of aggressive behaviour already mentioned or (and this is the majority) they simply have nothing to say. Church leaders are gradually coming to realize that the styles of church we have inherited from a past dominated by modernist ways of doing things fail to connect with today's wider culture.[1] But we need more than cosmetic changes to attract outsiders. A major reason for the Church's failure to connect with spiritual searchers is that all too often the churches we now have are actually disempowering people from effective engagement with others in creative mission. Without that, the Church in the West simply has no future. No amount of arguing can change the statistics, and though the precise figures vary from one country to another the overall trend is very firmly downwards and the situation is now so dire that more than one major denomination could disappear from the UK scene sometime in the decade between 2020 and 2030, if not sooner. Though some Christians retain an extraordinary degree of faith in the face of all this, looking and praying for some renewal of church fortunes, there is no obvious reason why we should expect the Church to survive in the West. For roughly the first thousand years of Christian history, the epicentre of the faith was around the shores of the Mediterranean, and North Africa was home to some of the most influential theologians in the early centuries. The next thousand years saw the centre move north and west, and North Africa became a Christian wasteland in the process. Could it be that we are now on the cusp of another global movement in which the future of the Church belongs not to Western culture at all, but to the lands of the southern hemisphere and the developing world? Actually, it is already happening.[2]

Having laid such great emphasis here on the *missio Dei*, I would not wish to deny that divine initiatives might change the situation. But there are some aspects of church life that are so obviously contributing to the present crisis that it would require a massive and suicidal act of denial for church leaders to imagine that there is nothing that can be done by those of us who are still left in the churches. Those who resist change are living in cloud-cuckoo land, because the church is already changing, whether we like it or not. In my lifetime, it has gone from being a vibrant spiritual community at the centre of civic life to being on the margins, from being an all-age community to being largely the preserve of old people, and from being a place of nurture and spiritual growth for children to being a prison from which they escape as soon as they are old enough to make their own choices. The central question for church leaders to ask is not, 'Will we change?' but 'Are we willing to take the initiative to become the agents of the sort of intentional change that will reflect and grow out of the values of the gospel?' The question of children and young people highlights the problem quite precisely. For while it is certainly the case that a large (and growing) percentage of Western populations has no living connection with or knowledge of the church at all, it is still the case that Christian people have their own children and grandchildren. Even now, with much diminished overall numbers, the ability to retain the children of Christian parents and nurture them to adult faith would make an enormous difference to the future prospects of the Church. In fact, it would totally transform things and could potentially turn serious decline into modest growth, more or less overnight.[3] When those who have been brought up within the church are leaving as soon as they can, something is very fundamentally wrong at the heart of things. We cannot dismiss their rejection as the incoherent response of those who do not really know what the church stands for. They do know what it is about, and that is the very reason why they leave. In the process of doing so, not only do they change the age profile of local congregations, but their leaving also disempowers their own families as credible witnesses – for who can with any conviction invite others to follow a path that has not worked for their own children? Addressing this honestly might well turn out to be the one thing that could make the most significant contribution of all to the renewal of the Church in Western culture – not only by reflecting on why Christian young people leave the Church, but also by creating safe spaces in which their parents and grandparents find healing for their personal pain about all this. The two aspects can probably be dealt with in the same way, because it is the McDonaldized control mechanisms of church life that both alienate young people and also prevent people of their parents' and grandparents' generations from addressing their own vulnerabilities in a redemptive way. If traditional churches in the West are to have any significant future, the creation of open-ended and safe spaces in which people of all sorts can explore what it means to follow Jesus will be absolutely central.

A personal story

In order to root this in human experience, here is a personal story that makes the point far more effectively than I could by talking in abstractions. I came across it in an issue of *SageWoman* that focused on the theme of 'prayer and invocation', and it is reproduced here with the permission of its author, Lee Pelham Cotton:

> Home from work on a hot summer's day, I feed the cats, kiss the dog and get dinner started. My husband is working late tonight. I pour a cold drink and settle into the armchair under the oak tree. I take a deep breath, and then another. And thus begins my prayer . . .
>
> Like so many, the word 'prayer' carries a cartload of baggage for me. In the church I attended in my teens, someone else did the praying. I sat very quietly with my head bowed, hands clasped, eyes closed. I opened the hymnbook to the proper page and sang the hymns posted on the chalkboard, hymns someone else selected, and listened to the sermon, someone else's words on the spiritual.
>
> The walls were pristine white; the carpet was scarlet and spotless. The candles burned without smoke; the only fragrance was a faint odor of Lysol [disinfectant] hanging in the air. The windows were translucent glass through which the rays of the sun shone but weakly.
>
> I never felt a connection with the holy under such conditions. It was like being in school: who you were was being subordinated to what others wished you to become. Your creativity and talents were definitely not encouraged. You didn't have to do a thing, for all had been set into motion eons before. Your role was to be a passive, silent witness. I did not feel blessed by this. I felt vaguely ashamed, and very small and alone.[4]

This story is by no means unique. Every research project that has enquired into the reasons why people fail to connect meaningfully with the church has highlighted exactly these same themes. Alan Jamieson's book *A Churchless Faith* is full of similar stories, drawn from south-east England and New Zealand; as also is

William Hendricks's earlier study of people who leave church in the USA; and the same thing is true of the work by Philip Richter and Leslie Francis entitled *Gone but not Forgotten*, while the Kendal Project headed up by Paul Heelas and Linda Woodhead came up with the same picture.[5]

Before considering some of the specific issues that arise out of the story recounted above, it will be worthwhile making a couple of general points. There is no evidence here that would in any reasonable way justify the sort of paranoid Christian responses to New Spirituality that we looked at in a previous chapter. What Lee Pelham Cotton reports about her own experience is not motivated by anger or hatred of Christians or churches. On the contrary, the tone not only of the paragraphs quoted here but also of the entire article is more one of sad resignation to the fact that a faith which worked for previous generations no longer seems to have meaningful connections for those who are searching for spiritual reality in today's world. It is equally clear that this concern is not born out of a generally cynical or negative attitude about life in general. On the contrary, all the evidence indicates that those who are concerned about such matters are prepared to commit themselves to a profound, and often costly, search for positive spiritual values that will not only empower us to be the people we are intended to be, but that will also create community and offer healing and forgiveness to those who are broken. Moreover, while there will always be exceptions to every rule, the terms of reference within which this spiritual search is taking place are often reflective of Christian values. Though the story quoted here does not do so, a theme that comes across repeatedly in other research is of committed individuals who leave the church because they want to be faithful to the gospel, and they have concluded that the two things are incompatible.[6] It is clearly not an exaggeration to say that the church seems to alienate the very people who, if they found it to be a place that resonated with their sense of spiritual search, would not only be in the church but would be among its most active members. If this pattern continues to be replicated, it will inevitably speed up the cycle of decline: by chasing away the spiritual searchers, the church is actually contributing to its own demise because not only does it lose them but by definition those who are then left will be the ones who feel less attuned to the searchers' questions and will be correspondingly less inclined to want to connect with this significant section of the population.

But let us return to the story from Lee Pelham Cotton, because the way it is expressed highlights some major issues for church leaders:

Non-participation

This is a major issue here: 'someone else did the praying . . . someone else's word on the spiritual'. The major 'activity' was not activity at all, but consisted of passive attendance, giving assent to a mediated, disconnected and ultimately irrelevant understanding of what it meant to be spiritual. It is worth noticing that this woman was not necessarily looking for group activities. In fact, one of the things that is strikingly absent from her account of churchgoing is an indication that anyone else was there apart from her and the preacher. Community was not on that church's agenda – something that is not altogether unfamiliar to churchgoers today. Yet despite the solitariness of the experience, there was no space to be herself, nor for any personal engagement with the disciplines of spirituality which she later came to value so highly.

Compartmentalization

Intrinsic to the life of this church was the assumption that worship and real life were segregated from one another, with no obvious connection between the two. In order to be 'spiritual' in this context, it was necessary to go somewhere else, into the church building, for that was the approved and designated place for religious practice. Paradoxically, as Lee Pelham Cotton's story unfolds in the rest of her article, she recalls how as a teenager she had been pleasantly shocked by a Sunday School teacher who took her class outside and told them that God was not imprisoned in the building. But that realization had not rehabilitated church for her. On the contrary, it opened up new avenues of spiritual exploration that did not depend on buildings. Reading her recollections of that church, it is not difficult to see why. For whether by design or accident, this place that was designated for worship was definitely not of this world. Nor did it manifest a sense of mystery that would have allowed it to be representative of another world. It was just that it was disconnected from the world outside the doors of the building ('the windows were translucent . . . sun shone but weakly'). The majority of intentional spiritual searchers have no problem about connecting with another world of transcendent reality, but they have real questions about any form of belief that does not relate to the actual world in which we live our everyday lives. This sense of disconnection from the real world is highlighted by the almost clinical nature of the building itself. The description here makes it sound more like a laboratory than a spiritual space, with its bare walls, spotless carpets, smokeless candles and the pervasive fragrance of cleaning products – all of these things sending out a subliminal message that the outside world is dirty or 'unclean' in some way.

McDonaldization

This was not a liberating environment. Quite the reverse: it was a place where 'your creativity and talents were definitely not encouraged'. An individual's uniqueness was buried under the weight of a homogenizing environment in which everyone had to look like peas in a pod. It reminds me of the statement by George Ritzer that grabbed my attention when I first came across his book *The McDonaldization of Society*: 'Human beings, equipped with a wide array of skills and abilities, are asked to perform a limited number of highly simplified tasks over and over . . . forced to deny their humanity and act in a robot-like manner.'[7] For me, that one single sentence had 'church' written all over it, and as I reflected further on its implications I realized that most churches are indeed McDonaldized in the way he describes, characterized by social structures of efficiency, calculability, predictability, and control.[8] The damaging nature of this way of being is highlighted by the emphasis on shame in Lee Cotton's account: all the memories associated with her teenage religious practices left her 'vaguely ashamed, and very small and alone'. In theological terms, she had no sense of being a person made in the image of God. Instead, she found church to be isolating and alienating.

Different people tell different stories, but these threads are sufficiently common to form a launch pad for further reflection. It is not hard to see why so many people now distinguish between religion and spirituality. Shirley Maclaine complains that 'Your religions teach religion, not spirituality'[9] though it is U2's Bono who articulated one of the most quotable descriptions of the problem in an interview with the website www.beliefnet.com in February 2001:

> I often wonder if religion is the enemy of God. It's almost like religion is what happens when the Spirit has left the building. God's Spirit moves through us and the world at a pace that can never be constricted by any one religious paradigm. I love that. You know, it says somewhere in the scriptures that the Spirit moves like a wind – no one knows where it's come from or where it's going. The Spirit is described in the Holy Scriptures as much more anarchic than any established religion credits.[10]

His recollection of the Bible's teaching was right, of course, as anyone who is familiar with the Fourth Gospel will recall (see John 3:8).

Different types of people

Before reflecting on all this in more theological vein, it will be worthwhile thinking about what might be happening here in cultural terms. It is easy enough to be negative about the Church. Indeed it is arguable that an over-emphasis on the problems is actually exacerbating the situation by heightening the sense of failure already felt by many church leaders, but without offering any practical way out of the difficulties. I believe that the kind of failings in the Church that have been highlighted here are undoubtedly real, and addressing them will be absolutely crucial to the future prospering of the Church in Western societies. But they are not the whole picture, for when all is said and done the churches we now have clearly meet the spiritual needs of at least *some* people, otherwise no one at all would be in them. Putting it that way, however, highlights the fundamental underlying issue, which is that most churches only appeal to one kind of person. In *The McDonaldization of the Church*, I identified seven people groups to whom the Church could and should relate: the desperate poor, hedonists, spiritual searchers, traditionalists, secularists, corporate achievers, and the apathetic.[11] This taxonomy has been widely acclaimed, not least by sociologist George Ritzer,[12] and more than one reviewer has agreed with the opinion that this is 'a compelling analysis of the social and cultural groups the Churches need to reach if they are to reverse their current alarming decline'.[13] I suggested that, to varying degrees, most churches have a surfeit of traditionalists, corporate achievers and the apathetic. These people groups were never intended to be mutually exclusive, and I indicated at the time how a corporate achiever might also be a hedonist, or an apathetic person might also be a traditionalist, and so on. Nor were these categories intended to form the basis of any sort of value judgement. I was not implying that there is anything wrong with being (for example) a traditionalist. Indeed, in terms of the current profile of most churches it seems to me that traditionalists and the attitudes they bring with them are both the strength and weakness of many local congregations. In spite of the paranoia and anguished hand-wringing among denominational leaders, I believe that the church might actually be doing quite well among those people with whom it can connect. The way in which statistics about church life are currently gathered offers no way of either confirming or denying that hunch. Actually, the way information is gathered is itself a part of the bigger problem, because almost all official figures only count people who attend Sunday services whereas changing lifestyles mean that, even among those people who are regularly active in congregational life, a growing number make their most significant contribution outside of Sunday worship. However we count them, though, the key challenge in relation to the future of the Church is that the sort of people who find church life most appealing are almost certainly a dwindling group in the wider population, and in particular, the social agenda is not being set by them today.

Within that wider population, the spiritual searchers are an especially important group, not just because they are growing, but because in socio-economic terms they are the people who in the past provided lay leadership for the church. Now they are more likely to be found heading up single-issue pressure groups. As I speak with such people, it seems to me that they have not rejected the gospel, rather that it is not possible for them to hear it because most Christians know how to be church only for a different sort of person. An ancient and often repeated liturgy declares that worship is 'for all people, at all times and in all places'. Whatever may have been the case in the past, today that is little more than an idealistic aspiration. Quite apart from bigger theological and liturgical questions about what might qualify as meaningful worship for post-modern people, what the church now does is accessible only to some of the people, at very limited times and in sometimes inhospitable places. And that just describes the physical, outward manifestation of church life! At a conceptual level, much of it might as well be on a different planet because there is little or no shared language between the concerns of New Spirituality and what Christians regard as important, for all the reasons that were outlined in the previous chapter. There is a legitimate debate to be had about how the central core of the gospel should be contextualized within different cultural environments. But our unthinking embrace of a 'one size fits all' attitude has not helped to push that debate forward. It is, up to a point, a comfortable position because it requires minimal adjustments by those who are already Christians: to become part of the church, other people have to change to become like us. But a way of being church that connects with only certain types of people is not biblical, it is not incarnational – and arguably, it is not fully Christian. In order to become all those things, the church itself will have to undergo a significant conversion experience.

Another way of approaching this matter has recently been highlighted by Dr Charlotte Craig of the University of Wales in Bangor, with research into the psychological type preferences of churchgoers in the UK (predominantly, though not exclusively, England and Wales). This research was based on responses from almost 3000 churchgoers, representing nine different denominational traditions, and utilized the Francis Psychological Type Scales,[14] a method which is based on the pioneering work of Carl

Gustav Jung (and also operationalized by the Myers-Briggs Type Indicator).[15] The findings from this study are very revealing in relationship to the Church's predicament in today's culture, and show that in three out of four categories certain preferences are over-represented among churchgoers when compared with the wider population. In terms of relationships, most church people (57 per cent) turned out to be more likely to be introverts than extraverts, preferring to keep themselves to themselves, enjoying working alone more than with other people, hardly ever going to parties, and generally feeling uncomfortable in socially interactive situations. This inevitably creates a certain sort of ambience in church, appealing to those who 'feel at home walking into a quiet and meditative space and prefer to slip off quietly afterwards. They like being left to their own space during the service. When a newcomer turns up they wait for that person to make the first move.'[16] When it comes to the way in which we use information, this research demonstrated an overwhelming preference among 79 per cent of Christians for down-to-earth, conventional, and practical measures that will maintain the status quo, rather than a more imaginative approach (probably combined with creative interaction) that would draw its inspiration from a vision of how things might be, and might then seek to initiate the change that would help to turn the dreams into reality. Correspondingly, most church members (61 per cent) like to maintain a sense of peace and harmony, rather than taking tough decisions that might cause dissension. For such people, it is more important to maintain humane and caring attitudes towards others than it is to apply logic and reason to matters of church policy or doctrine. In the light of all that, it is little cause for surprise that an even bigger proportion of church people (84 per cent) generally like routine and organization, along with certainty and structure rather than change and spontaneity – something that correlates very well with my previous work in applying the McDonaldization thesis to church life. Discussion of these preferences in relation to church structures could legitimately be extended in several directions. Here, I wish to stick with the missiological significance of these findings, which is highlighted when these attitudes are compared with the norms for the wider population.[17] In terms of the UK population (and the same will almost certainly be true for other Western populations), the only one of these four categories in which churchgoers' preferences show no significant difference from the wider population is in relation to the way we perceive and use information.

When we connect this with the trajectory of understandings of what is 'spiritual' that was proposed in chapter 2, it suggests that the way church now is connects very happily with the middle ground of 'discipline', and to a lesser extent with what I called the 'lifestyle' end of the spectrum – but scarcely at all with the 'enthusiasm' end where there is so much energy. As was emphasized in that context, these are just different ways of connecting with that spirituality which is endemic to being human – so in that sense, there is nothing wrong with the sort of spiritual preferences expressed by those people who are now in church. What is problematic is that this represents only a small – and probably shrinking — group within the wider population.

Signposts to a better future

What factors will we need to take account of for a church to connect effectively with those whom I have called intentional spiritual searchers? I deliberately put it like that, because to provide some sort of model would be to propose just another McDonaldized form of spiritual community – which would suffer from all the drawbacks of the rationalized congregations we now have. The one thing we can say for certain is that there is no single blueprint that can be applied universally. There are many ways of being church that will be faithful to the gospel. Some of them will continue to be institutional, many more will be spontaneous and informal. But some things seem clear. The days when McDonaldized forms of church could be dominant are over, and if we really believe the first page of the Bible, and celebrate the fact that we are all, in our amazing diversity, people made in God's image, then that should be a cause for rejoicing, not for regret. Having said that, I believe we can identify some compass points for the future. The imagery of finding a direction, and journeying along that pathway, is not only thoroughly biblical, but is also useful in reflecting on the difference between the Christian past and the future to which God now calls us.

In the past, our forebears were concerned to provide believers with a detailed street map that would show every step of the way. In doing so, they reflected the preferences of their age, whether that was the fourth-century Roman empire or the nineteenth-century British empire. But highly detailed maps can sometimes be more of a hindrance than a help.[18] This book began life as lectures delivered in London towards the end of 2004. In travelling to a big city like London, it is generally advisable to use the public transportation systems. But on that occasion, my wife and I stayed in London for a full month, which meant we had much more baggage than usual, and so we decided to make the journey by car. At the time we were based in the north of Scotland, which was a long enough journey, but perfectly straightforward until we reached the northern suburbs of London and had to find our way through the city centre in order to reach our final destination, which was to the south of the city. We were of course well prepared – too well prepared, as it turned out. Before leaving home, we had visited a website looking for road maps, and had downloaded driving directions which, the providers assured us, would guide us with unfailing accuracy along every mile of the journey in such a way that it would be impossible to get lost. That was no idle boast: the instructions even told us which way to turn as we left our own driveway! But in the event, these directions turned out to be so detailed in their description of the various landmarks we would see, and the turns we needed to make, that the sort of detail that we thought would give clear guidance turned out to be so confusing that it was almost useless. The problem was that too much information was provided, with every nook and cranny of the streets described in such detail that, faced with the busyness of city streets, it was impossible to take it all in, let alone navigate by it. We never actually got lost, in the sense of not knowing where we were, but in the end we reached our destination through a combination of common sense, a general idea of direction, and a good dose of intuition. That strikes me as a good paradigm for the spiritual life. We need a compass, not a street map. The difference between them is simple, but crucial: a street map gives directions, whereas a compass gives direction. Some will no doubt find this analogy too vague and woolly, so it is important for me to add that in order to be authentically Christian I believe that the future Church needs to take its direction by reference to the same compass point as those who went before us. When we turn to one of the most fundamental of those compass points from the past – the Bible – it is significant that it too gives direction, not directions. This can frustrate those who search in vain for prescriptive statements, but in reality it is one of the key reasons why a book so ancient is still a potent source of spiritual wisdom in the twenty-first century. Tomorrow's Christians can never hope to replicate the circumstances of biblical times: to try and do so would be a denial of the essentially incarnational nature of Christian faith, which requires that in order to stay the same the gospel must be changing all the time. What I believe we should be, however, is continuous with the past – otherwise, how can we claim to be authentically 'Christian'? The authentic Church of the future will be less about reinventing ourselves, and more about rediscovering a heritage that we have lost sight of.

What are the essential compass points to which we now should be looking? These are grouped under different headings here, but that is mostly a matter of convenience that will hopefully make the discussion easier to follow. In reality, they are all interconnected, and are different facets of what is in effect the same fundamental question.

Mystery

We need to reaffirm the church as a locus of mystery, a place where God is at the centre. By saying that, I do not mean to imply that God is not present everywhere (if it were not for the wider *missio Dei* this entire discussion would be pointless), but there can be little doubt that the emphasis on the rational and cognitive aspects of faith that dominated the last two or three centuries has ignored (and sometimes denied) the transcendent dimension of the Christian tradition. We can trace the consequences of this tendency in a number of ways.

One of the most obvious manifestations of this is **that the**

appropriate balance between beliefs and experience has been disturbed, in such a way that we have elevated dogma at the expense of discipleship. This is to get things the wrong way round. Theology in its most pristine form starts not with rational reflection, but with discipleship. We are called to follow Jesus, and 'theology' is what emerges as we reflect on the meaning of the experience. The earliest disciples followed (and were, therefore, 'real' disciples) long before they had any 'beliefs' about Christology, salvation, the sacraments, or indeed any of the other things we imagine to be so central today (Mark 1:16-20).[19] Moreover, the same pattern was repeated in the life of the earliest Church's greatest theologian, St Paul, whose meeting with the risen Christ on the Damascus road was the source and inspiration for even his most abstract thinking, as he unpacked the significance of what had come to him first and foremost as a transcendent experience of the risen Christ.[20] To describe them in today's jargon, these people were reflective practitioners.[21] It was understandable that, in the endeavour to make Christian belief more rationally accessible in a culture where rationality was highly prized, our forebears should have emphasized the cognitive aspects of faith. But in the process of doing so, it seems that something was lost that was actually central to the tradition. The cultural changes leading to the emergence of a so-called post-modern culture are not only inviting us to revisit our historic roots to identify those core values of the gospel that will offer the sort of direction mentioned earlier, but they have also created a world in which the mysterious and the transcendent have been rehabilitated, as much through the research of physicists and neurobiologists as through the practice of those who intentionally seek out the company of angels or search for other hidden mysteries that might shed light on the meaning of life. Leith Anderson has expressed it well with his comment that, 'The old paradigm taught that if you have the right teaching, you will experience God. The new paradigm says that if you experience God, you will have the right teaching.'[22] This is one of those 'altars to unknown gods' that were discussed in the previous chapter, and where the concerns of post-modern spiritual searchers and our own roots in the New Testament coalesce in ways that point to new challenges and opportunities in relation to contextualizing the gospel in today's world. Any message that aspires to be incarnational in contemporary culture cannot ignore the significance of what is mysterious and transcendent.

Another consequence of the unthinking accommodation of the gospel to modernist values is that **the Christian world view has been unhelpfully secularized** by imbibing somewhat uncritically the attitudes and belief systems of Cartesian science and philosophy. In the light of this, it is easy to see why some Christians would like to insist that both the medium and the message must be completely unchanging in terms of both values and presentation, and that anything less is likely to amount to little more than a short-sighted pandering to changing cultural fads and fancies. A concern to contextualize the gospel in different cultures will always be a risky business, for how do you know when the expression of the message in a particular cultural form is having the effect of corrupting the underlying values rather than communicating them? The honest answer is to admit that while we are engaged in the process we cannot really be certain of the answer to that. It is only as later generations can view particular cultural expressions of faith from the relative safety of a broader historical perspective that both the strengths and the weaknesses of what a given generation does can be brought into clearer focus. This will be as true for those of us who are attempting to embody the gospel in today's popular culture of post-modernity as it has been for our forebears in the past. For this reason alone, we ought to be benevolent in relation to those who have gone before us, recognizing that in the same circumstances we would probably have done the same things. It is easy to see how the marriage between Greek philosophy and Christian faith in the early centuries created creedal language that was all but incomprehensible for subsequent generations, and how the dualism that was central to such a world view helped to foster a peculiarly disembodied version of spirituality, especially when it was later combined with the individualism that was both a product of and a catalyst for the Protestant Reformation. But it would be foolish to imply that the effort to contextualize Christian faith in the culture of the Enlightenment was a fundamentally misguided endeavour. William Storrar has made a brave attempt to demonstrate that the Church 'married modernity . . . [only] for the best of missiological reasons', but this was not a marriage of equals, and in the event the gospel turned out to be very much a junior and subservient partner.[23] This can be traced not only in relation to the diminution of a sense of transcendence, which was our starting point here, but also in the way that the Church of that period embraced with some enthusiasm the status and perceived social standing that the export of Western ways of doing things seemed to offer. A similar dichotomy emerges in the study of spirituality in Kendal reported by Heelas and Woodhead, who take it for granted that by definition church life is concerned with 'pre-packaged life-as values, beliefs, or injunctions'.[24] While they are hardly telling us something new, from a theological angle we must ask a different question, namely is that *really* what church is supposed to be? Or is that not a corrupted and disempowering version of the faith that has been created by a McDonaldizing mindset that in turn represents a contextualization in the wrong direction, as the values of the culture have become embedded in the Church rather than the gospel having become a transformational element within the culture? A world view that is faithful to the historic roots of the Christian tradition will be significantly different both from the rationalistic attitudes that dominated the world of modernity, and also from the irrational attitudes that frequently surface in the culture of post-modernity. By rationalistic I mean the outlook which operates with a fixed view of what is possible, and says there is nothing worth knowing that cannot be discerned purely by rational, logical – and therefore predictable – thought processes. That assumption has led to the development of a fragmented, reductionist way of understanding human nature, and deserves to be discarded. It is however deeply entrenched in the Western Christian psyche, which means that questioning it will be a more complicated matter than merely quoting a few Bible texts. The people who are most represented in the Church tend to be dismissive of anything that does not follow the 'laws' of strict logic (logic defined, that is, on the pattern of ancient Greek thinking). The issue has been exacerbated for many by the way in which some representatives of New Spirituality have reacted against rationality in such an extreme fashion that it seems they automatically distrust anything that makes logical sense. Bhagwan Shree Rajneesh went so far as to claim that rational, analytical thinking will actually prevent a person from achieving spiritual enlightenment: 'It is not that the intellect sometimes misunderstands. Rather, the intellect always misunderstands. It is not that the intellect sometimes errs; it is that the intellect is the error . . .'[25] Influenced by such notions, increasing numbers of people assume that if something seems to make sense by what look like the inherited (i.e. Greek) definitions of logic, it must automatically be suspect. The fact that this rejection of rationality also tends to feed into the sort of deconstruction of Christianity which was highlighted in the first chapter merely compounds the problem for many Christians.[26]

Shirley Maclaine quotes the well-known channeler Kevin Ryerson asking, 'Did what came through *feel* right? They've told me to just trust my feelings. There's nothing else you can do once you begin to ask these questions.'[27] A few pages later she adds, 'The thing is it all seems to be about "feeling", not thinking.'[28] Recent Western culture has often preferred reason over emotion and feelings. But feelings by themselves are unlikely to be any more useful than rationality by itself. We need a more holistic paradigm that takes into account all the different ways in which we can 'know' things or people. To rely on feelings to the exclusion of reason is merely perpetuating the very same reductionist attitudes that the proponents of New Spirituality claim to dislike so much. To be fully human requires that feelings and reason work together in harmony.

Nevertheless, it is undeniable that **Christianity has tended to be much happier with reason than with emotion**. At a purely practical level, in order to cope with church, people need to be able to deal with abstract concepts through their mental processes, and those who more naturally operate in an intuitive, artistic, or creative way frequently complain about finding little that speaks to them. At the same time – and somewhat paradoxically – there has been a tendency to be rational about faith in a less than thoroughgoing way, so that tough questions also tend to be avoided, or their importance played down. I remember a conversation with an intelligent young woman looking for a church in a city to which she had recently moved, and telling me that the churches she had visited 'would be alright if you left your brains at the door'. That phenomenon itself is a product of an over-rationalized approach to faith, that prioritizes a propositional way of articulating truth, and expresses varying degrees of uneasiness not only with the imagination, but with other non-cognitive things such as images and symbols. Some of my conversation partners tell me that I am over-sensitive to this because I have lived for much of my life in Scotland, where there has indeed been a great historical emphasis on the rationality of Christian faith. But Donal Dorr, an Irish priest with worldwide experience of missionary work, identifies exactly the same problem and suggests that 'one major reason why many people seldom think of God is because for them God has been reduced to being the essence of reasonableness – and that seems rather dull and unattractive'.[29] In contrast, Jesus (repeating teaching that was already deeply rooted in the Hebrew tradition) promoted a holistic image of discipleship when he spoke of responding to God with 'heart, soul, mind and strength' (Mark 12:30, quoting Deuteronomy 6:4-5).

Probably as a by-product of all these things, **Christians tend to be uncomfortable with the mystical/numinous/supernatural**. Not all those who speak the language of New Spirituality have a strong belief in some kind of spiritual reality lying beyond this world, but a considerable number do, wherever they might be located on the spectrum of lifestyle, discipline, and enthusiasm. The whole question of direct personal perception of the divine is, in varying ways, of growing concern to an increasing proportion of the population. The precise way in which this is described seems less important than how Christians will relate to it, which is why I am happy to use words like mystical, numinous, and supernatural as more or less interchangeable. Discovering what Christians think about any of this is not straightforward, and the uneasiness that is displayed when such matters are raised readily convinces others that the Church is so thoroughly locked into a rationalist-materialist thought pattern that, at best, its opinions are irrelevant and, at worst, probably most Christians either have no belief in this sort of thing, or have no idea what to believe. I remember having a conversation with one of the world's leading exponents of New Spirituality, who had been raised in an ecumenical household and had a shrewd understanding of the typical Christian mindset (one of her parents was a Roman Catholic, the other a Baptist). Now in mid-life and explaining to me why New Spirituality made more sense than the Church, she highlighted what for her was a meaningless contradiction: 'The Church is full of rationalists. I know Christians who would fight to the death to defend the belief that Jesus performed miracles, but then will fight just as vigorously to deny that there is any such thing as the miraculous in today's world.' She was describing the classic Reformed evangelical position, which to her was basically a rationalist viewpoint with an unexpected twist in it: the numinous is all right, so long as it is firmly in the past and has no immediate connection to life here and now. That made no sense to her, not only because she herself had had many mystical experiences, but also because she found this sense of the numinous almost everywhere in the Bible. In addition to the stories about Jesus, she highlighted Moses' experience at the burning bush (Exodus 3:1-14), Elijah's experience of the 'still small voice' (1 Kings 19:3-18), Ezekiel being mystically transported from Babylon to Jerusalem and back in what seemed to her like astral projection (Ezekiel 8:3), and Paul's claim to have had what sounded very much like out-of-body experiences (2 Corinthians 12:1-6).

This is one of the places where the thinking of the European Enlightenment had a particularly profound impact on Christian beliefs. In the face of a dominant materialist view of reality, any world view that had a place for the numinous was soon relegated to the mythological dustbin as a hangover from a primitive and unsophisticated world that had apparently gone forever. The dominance of this opinion, in theology and philosophy in particular, produced whole generations of church leaders who came to understand their own faith heritage in reductionist terms, and who regarded spiritual experience as little more than a branch of social anthropology, to be studied (if at all) only as a historical curiosity. For people who were also committed to a colonialist mentality, it was irrelevant to note that the majority of the world's people at all times and places have always believed in this sort of thing: the fact that modernity was rejecting it was just one more proof of the superiority of the Western mindset over the world view of other races. The insistent rise of New Spirituality (especially in terms of discipline and enthusiasm) has challenged all that. It has even, on occasion, argued that this loss of awareness of another world has contributed to the collapse of our culture. It might be imagined that the rise of the charismatic movement has in some way counteracted this, and insofar as there is evidence of any part of the Church holding its own in the present culture of spiritual search, then the statistics give some slight encouragement to this view.[30] In their study of the spiritual life of Kendal, Paul Heelas and Linda Woodhead also concluded that what they called 'congregations of experiential difference' (which roughly correspond to charismatic churches) were the only ones likely to have much of a future.[31] It is instructive to note, however, that they reach that conclusion not on the basis of the theology of such groups, but because they regard them as giving a rather high priority to people and their felt needs. The reality is that such churches tend to display the same alienating features as other types of church. McDonaldized ways of being are not difficult to identify here, especially predictability ('all will speak in tongues', or some equivalent) and control (charismatic 'shepherding' structures can make the Vatican look radical and liberal by comparison) – but efficiency and calculability are also not hard to find, especially among Christian missionary organizations that prioritize numbers of converts and speed of operation. Throughout the 1990s groups such as AD 2000 and DAWN ('Disciple a Whole Nation') bombarded Christians with the claim that their patented methodologies would ensure the evangelization of the whole world by the start of the twenty-first century by delivering the maximum results in minimum time, using the most efficient methods of operation. Charismatic churches face just as many difficulties as others when it comes to contextualizing their message effectively for spiritual searchers. Moreover, the sort of aggressive attitudes toward spiritual searchers which were examined in the previous chapter have to a large extent been engendered by the intensely dualistic world view that tends to predominate in such circles. An understanding of human nature that operates on this sort of 'them and us' paradigm will need to undergo considerable revision if it is to connect in any missiologically meaningful way with the kind of scientific research into the nature of spirituality which we considered in chapter 2. One does not need to hold to a strictly dualistic world view in order to value the numinous, and research into different dimensions of reality is showing that the cosmos itself is more complex and mysterious than previous generations imagined to be possible.

Community

A second major challenge in this context is the need to rediscover how the church can be a place of community, nurture, and personal growth. This is another topic that also invites us to return to our historic roots in a way that easily relates to one of the key concerns of contemporary culture. In a fragmented society, people are looking for a place to belong. We search out places of safety, where we can be empowered rather than stifled, and where we can be open with others, acknowledging our needs and inadequacies with an expectation of support rather than a fear of condemnation. We all long to find acceptance for who we are rather than having to conform to images of who other people think we should be. This will inevitably be challenging – more for some than others – because it requires us to value one another as persons made in God's image, regardless of class, gender, ethnicity, sexuality, or other characteristics that may appear to divide us. Heelas and Woodhead's research identified the 'face-to-face relational nature' of much contemporary spiritual practice as being especially attractive to people who take the spiritual search most seriously,[32] and further comment that 'What matters is growing oneself through the experiences of associational activities . . . The spiritual dimension is (basically) understood as the dimension at which all life connects, and where the individual realizes her or his true nature in relationship with the "whole".'[33] This is of profound importance not only for church as community, but also in relation to what happens in worship. The importance attached to meaningful community in what Heelas and Woodhead call the 'holistic domain' might suggest that in some of these contexts kingdom concerns are more highly valued than in some churches. It is certainly the case that the creation of open community seems to be especially problematic for Christians.

Some of the reasons for this might well relate to the matter of personality types already discussed, though I suspect that another key factor is likely to be a lack of openness about our own vulnerabilities. A willingness to handle weakness and vulnerability is nevertheless one of the hallmarks of meaningful community. To belong in a place with confidence, we need to have the assurance that we can be accepted for who we are, and affirmed in our desire for transformation to become the people we most want to be. It has sometimes been implied that Christians need to have their own lives in order before they can effectively witness to others. Jesus never called disciples to be perfect or infallible, but to be true to themselves and to the gospel, and in the process of doing so to invite others to join them in the struggle to be human, spiritual, and Christian that is part of life's journey. Evangelism is more about inviting others to join us on the journey, because we share the same questions, than it is about selling people the 'right' answers to life's problems. Once more, the New Testament insistently calls us back to this emphasis, with many images that depict the spiritual life as a process, and its extensive use of the idea (if not always the actual language) of 'new birth'. Previous generations often preferred to use the imagery of death to describe the Christian life, perhaps because that was the one reality with which men were most familiar through their participation in warfare (and I do mean 'men', for they were the ones who not only fought the battles but also determined the theological agenda). Death imagery inevitably directs us to the mistakes of the past, and invites us to apportion blame, whereas the imagery of birth and new life invites us to look to future possibilities of who we might become, and to trust in the transforming power of God's grace.[34] The mention here of 'men' is also likely to be more relevant than many Christians would like to think. For despite many efforts to change things, the underlying structures of much church life still operate in a very male way. This is hardly surprising, because historically they were established by men, and reflect male ways of doing things. But it does highlight the fact that the creation of a more inclusive community is not going to be accomplished through cosmetic moves that allow women and other previously excluded groups into a man's world, but requires that we engage in a more far-reaching appraisal of how things operate. Church people tend to think of this as an internal organizational matter, but it is in fact a missiological concern, for as Donal Dorr points out, 'if women's spirituality were taken seriously, [church] would be more flexible and less legalistic . . . less narrowly intellectual and more experiential'[35] – and these are all issues that tend to make the church inaccessible to spiritually concerned people.

In relation to contextualizing the gospel in contemporary culture, there are several key questions emerging from this. First of all is the need to **develop a relevant theology of the human person and of meaningful models of spiritual growth**. People feel disjointed, out of tune with their physical environment, out of touch with other people, and even unable to come to terms with themselves. There is a lot of hurt around, and many wounded people who are looking for personal healing. This has become a major catalyst in the growth of lifestyle spirituality, because this is the point at which we become aware of the damaging nature of so much human experience. It is in the events of daily life, what happens in relationships in both the workplace and the home, that we are most acutely aware of issues of fragmentation, alienation, and lostness. In the effort to address such matters, lonely people look for other people with whom to congregate. Reference has already been made to Douglas Coupland's extraordinary ability to put into words some of the deepest aspirations of spiritual searchers, and the missiological imperative at this point is nowhere better expressed than in the comment made by a character in his novel *Microserfs* who observes that 'people without lives like to hang out with other people who don't have lives. Thus they form lives.'[36] We do not have to look far for evidence of such activity. On the one hand, we like our privacy and individuality, and value our own space to a much greater extent than previous generations.[37] But at the same time, we are far more likely than our grandparents' generation would have been to take the initiative and actively seek out opportunities to congregate. The rapid growth of health clubs, the rising audiences in cinemas, the increasing popularity of eating out rather than at home, and the burgeoning club culture (especially in Britain) are all symptomatic of this trend. In some of these situations, we congregate to engage in individualistic activities and the only communal aspect might be that we do things at the same time and place as other people. Health clubs and gyms would be an example of this, as also would the cinema or other theatrical contexts. But there is also a conscious spiritual search behind much of this. Sheryl Garratt believes that 'Clubs are the churches of the new millennium' and there is a good deal of evidence to support the claim.[38] In many cases it is literally true, as clubs in the UK are frequently housed in former church buildings, and their history as churches is often adapted to create a quasi sacramental ethos in the club. Moreover, much dance music specifically identifies the club scene as a spiritual community that is alternative to church. One of the most outstanding examples of this is the album *Sunday 8pm* by Faithless.[39] Several songs make unmistakable allusions to Bible stories, with titles like 'The Garden', 'Hour of Need', 'Take the long way Home', or 'Hem of his Garment', while 'God is a DJ' explicitly identifies club with church and describes the experience as one of healing, community-building, and transcendence. It might well be that such community as the club scene offers is fleeting and momentary, but it is real for as long as it lasts, and in today's fragmented society something – however transient – is always going to be better than nothing.[40]

This should hardly be a challenge for the Christian church. Jesus himself offered to make people whole, and throughout his teaching he described a life of fulfilment in which the divisions that cause pain can be healed. A holistic lifestyle features strongly on the pages of the New Testament. It is God's will. Yet the reality is that all too often church is just one more solitary experience among all the others (my previous use of the word 'congregating' was not coincidental). It is thirty years since Marion Leach Jacobsen published a book with the title *Crowded Pews and Lonely People*,[41] and while the pews are unlikely to be crowded now, the point still remains: it is all too possible for those who are lonely and broken to be offered only individualized experiences of God, even when they come to the church looking for spiritual nurturing. Charlotte Craig's research, mentioned earlier, highlights the same phenomenon, and while we need to take seriously the diversity of responses that might be offered by people of different personality types, if a privatized approach to faith and to friendship is the prevailing one, then the church has a big problem on its hands. Heelas and Woodhead's research draws attention to the very same issue, as they found that 'the paths to the holistic milieu which we have been dwelling on have one thing in common: relationality'.[42] I suggested in the first chapter that one reason why the wider culture now speaks more easily about spiritual needs can be traced to the popularity of reality TV shows like *Big Brother* and *The Jerry Springer Show*. That change of attitude also has a consequence for mission. Whether we like it or not, we now live in a society where people will share their most intimate secrets with anyone who is prepared to listen. In this environment, Christians who present themselves as privatized and introverted individuals will not come across in a very convincing way. On the contrary, a reticence to share our own stories of the spiritual journey is likely to be interpreted as a sign that we have nothing to say because we have nothing to share. There is of course a difference between forcing oneself on others in an aggressive fashion, and speaking of personal experience of God in a non-confrontational way, and in the past Christians have sometimes been guilty of the former. Fear of making the same mistake again no doubt prevents some from saying anything at all. But if the church is experienced not as a model of wholeness, but of separation, then ultimately we are denying the very gospel that we claim to hold dear.

Lack of personal openness also tends to perpetuate a kind of closet Christianity that can be found in local congregations of all denominations, where there is little evidence of any deep connection between Christian values and the lifestyles actually adopted by Christian people. Not only is this contrary to the teaching of Jesus and the example of the first disciples: it also has no appeal to those who are searching for a more integrated way of being. Anyone looking for a holistic answer to life's challenges will quite likely find the church to be too bland and undemanding. The days when people's needs for personal identity could be met through shallow relationships and glib moralistic advice have gone forever. Ian Wray speaks for many when he complains that Christianity has a 'traditional lack of therapeutic, by which I mean the lack of any real body of ideas and practices to help people change'. He goes on to observe that 'the near total absence of practical aids to human psychological and spiritual growth within Christianity left a vacuum which psychotherapy had to fill, based upon principles which it had to discover for itself'.[43] It is certainly the experience of many people that, when they encounter Christianity, they are more likely to be put down than to be lifted up. This is one of the points at which the New Spirituality has raised questions that demand an answer.

These concerns are more than common-sense pragmatism, for they also connect to more specifically theological matters. In particular, **we need to ask some serious questions about sin and blessing**. Significant numbers of Christians suffer from a low sense of self-esteem, and find themselves over-burdened with feelings of guilt and personal worthlessness. Having lived in the north of Scotland, I have seen the effects of this at first hand, as even lifelong believers tell me that they are still not worthy enough to take communion, let alone to engage in the mission of the church. In this cultural context at least, I suspect that what can look like unfriendliness and introversion stems less from innate personality traits, and more from these feelings of inadequacy – though if you are brought up to think like this, the two eventually coalesce and you become who other people say you should be. This theme of deliverance from guilt appears quite prominently in New Spirituality in all its various guises.

One popular way of addressing it is by affirming the power of positive thinking, and suggesting that 'You are what you make yourself'. Because this does not easily correlate with the lived experience of most of us, it is often explained by reference to arcane ideas about the origin and purpose of life here on earth. An extreme form of this would claim that knowing oneself in this life needs to begin with knowledge of past lives that we have lived. Though this is very much a minority interest, it is worth further reflection as it highlights in a somewhat extreme way both the attraction of and the problems with the notion that we are all who we have chosen to be. Shirley Maclaine outlines the world view behind this notion when she quotes a Swedish friend as saying,

> We are all spiritual beings. We just don't acknowledge it. We are spiritual beings of energy who happen to be in the physical body at the present time and Ambres [a channeled entity] is a spiritual being of energy who does not happen to be in the body right now. Of course, he is highly evolved, but then so are we. The difference is that we don't believe it.[44]

The way to access this knowledge is through connecting with some transcendent force, which she variously labels the 'Higher Self' (the core of personal spiritual being), though it might also be referred to as the superconscious, oversoul, God-Self, or Christ-Consciousness. This Higher Self is the way in which it is claimed we can identify our own true purpose, because it is through it that we originally chose to be who we now are, and therefore maintaining a regular connection with it will keep us focused on our priorities. It is no surprise that those who find life aimless and without meaning are readily attracted to therapists who claim to be able to put them in touch with this Higher Self. Not only can this become a way to resolve uncertainties and questions about the present by reference to what took place in past lives, but it also includes a claim to be able to answer the ultimate questions of meaning, by providing a fresh understanding of personal identity in relation to the entire cosmic scheme of things. There is an appealing and forceful message in all this, especially to people who suffer from a low self-esteem. For it suggests that they are actually very powerful and important beings, with the potential to do absolutely anything at all should they so choose.

This world view has obvious connections with belief in reincarnation, and to the uninitiated it can easily sound like a traditional Hindu or Buddhist belief. But it is so firmly rooted in Western individualism that its connection with the Indian tradition is highly tenuous, to say the least. Unlike the traditional Eastern view, which envisages the form in which a person returns to this world being directly related to their moral performance in previous lives, the claim here is that disembodied souls make their own personal choices as to who they will be, and what kind of circumstances they will encounter in life. These choices are allegedly made on the basis of their perceived spiritual needs at any given point. In his book *The Emerging New Age*, sociology professor J.L. Simmons puts it like this:

> the decision to be reborn is self-determined by each being in consultation with familiar spirits and, often, a small group of more knowledgeable counsellors. The rebirth is planned . . . Such plans include the circumstances of birth and a blueprint outline of the life to follow, so that certain experiences might provide the opportunity to learn certain lessons.[45]

That means that whoever a person is now, and whatever they might be experiencing, it is all happening because they chose that it would – including even such negative experiences as economic and social deprivation, personal oppression, marginalization, or a gruesome death. This is a world view with no moral fibre. The Eastern concept of reincarnation has been disembowelled, and combined with Western individualism in a way that appears to offer the best of all possible worlds, by providing the safety and security of a belief system that promises eternal existence, but without any demand for moral responsibility. It is not hard to see why such an outlook should be so popular, because it mirrors the values of late twentieth-century consumerism which I suggested in chapter 1 was one of the influences that facilitated the emergence of a popular quest for 'spiritual' answers to life's questions. But it is, in my opinion, deeply flawed, because of its inability to deal with the reality of evil and undeserved suffering. Worse, it implies that those who are suffering bring it on themselves, and the rest of us are thereby exonerated from taking their hardships seriously. This is indeed a form of spiritual capitalism.

Christians invariably have a robust attitude to the presence of sin in the world, but have regularly made the mistake of understanding sin in purely personal terms. No doubt this was a natural thing for some of our forebears to do, influenced by the individualism that has swept through the entire Western world in recent centuries. But when sin is seen in exclusively personal terms – especially when it becomes something that other people do, from which we need to rescue them, then it is all too easy for 'sin' to become little more than a form of social control through which we can judge people who seem not to be like us. This kind of unbiblical dualism has not only created a great deal of misery, it has also encouraged the acceptance of a shallow and theologically deviant understanding of both sin and salvation that is no more able to address the profound existential needs of people than the sort of opinions offered by those New Spirituality writers to whom I have just referred. In biblical terms, sin is not just an individual phenomenon – nor is that its primary reference point in Scripture. On the contrary, sin has a universal character that encompasses the breakdown of all relationships, not only between people themselves, but between people and the natural environment as well as between people and God. Whatever else may be said about him (and as I indicated in chapter 3, I am by no means uncritical of many of his ideas), Matthew Fox has done a great service to the Church by drawing attention to these questions, not least by highlighting the significance of 'original blessing' as the primary characteristic of God's relationship with humankind.[46] It is worthwhile pointing out here that this concern is also being voiced among more conservative mission thinkers today. Bryant Myers, writing in the *Evangelical Missions Quarterly*, put forward a powerful argument in favour of moving 'from a set of propositions to a narrative framework' for evangelism, adding that 'a genuinely holistic approach to mission begins with a strong creation theology' which he finds evidence of 'in the whole of Scripture'.[47] But this too drives us back to basic issues of community, for we do not experience God in a disembodied form, but through our experience of life. That is not to say that God cannot and does not intervene directly in people's lives, but

> it is very difficult for anybody to experience themselves as fully loved and accepted by God unless that person has had some similar experience of love and some degree of intimacy with one or more humans. We were not created

> as isolated individuals, called to find our lonely way to God . . . So we cannot expect to have an alternative route – one which enables us to by-pass the experience of human love and human intimacy in order to go directly to God.[48]

Jesus himself emphasized this when he told his disciples to 'love one another' (John 15:9-17). Unfortunately, as Dorr points out, the tendency of so many Christians to be judgemental and oppressive has meant that 'when people heard God is loving, the effect was not to enrich their understanding of God but rather to diminish their understanding of love'.[49] The medium is indeed the message.

Following on from that, I believe that **we need a more balanced view of God**. A major part of the legacy from the past concerns the Church's love of hierarchies. To a greater extent than most Christians seem prepared to acknowledge, the organizational and theological styles of traditional church structures find their justification in the patriarchal culture of European imperialism (and, beyond that, back via Christendom to ancient Rome). When imperialist expansion was high on the agenda of European nations – whether at the time of the Crusades, or the conquest of South America, or in the creation of the British empire – our forebears needed an imperialistic God, and the Church was not slow to supply the need. All too often, 'salvation' for the non-western world was the sharp end of a sword.[50] This tendency to over-emphasize just one aspect of the biblical picture of God (transcendence) has left the Church in a weak position when it comes to showing how the gospel relates to the rather different concerns of today's people, who on the whole are rejecting such images of 'power over' others, in favour of a more relational style of 'power in partnership' with others. When one recalls that at the heart of the gospel is not a God who became an all-conquering monarch, but a God who became a child, the perpetuation of overt images of top-down power is not merely culturally questionable, but theologically dubious as well. Though the Bible has its fair share of transcendent images, it also insists that Jesus is the most perfect revelation of the character of God, and in the process redefines who God is, in terms of weakness, vulnerability, and powerlessness. That image has been marginalized, for a variety of reasons. One has to do with the political power of the Church in the period of Christendom. Another is the unhealthy domination of Christian thinking by the uncritical adoption of a view of 'God' derived from Greek philosophy, in which all our theological outcomes need to be 'successful', and there is little or no space for tragedy and suffering, or for emotions like grief and failure. For people struggling to come to terms with the flaws in life, a God who is remote and 'successful' seems irrelevant – and uncaring. A God who understands suffering, and is able to accept failure while empowering those who are broken to move forward into new life, will speak more powerfully to today's people. In reality, this second image of God is absolutely central to the New Testament. But by creating the impression that the gospel is actually about the first, Christians can prevent spiritual searchers from effectively hearing what the gospel might have to say.

It is not difficult to expose the moral inadequacy of an exclusively immanent view of spiritual reality, such as we find in the monism of Shirley Maclaine or J.L. Simmons. But an exclusively transcendent understanding of God is no more able to deal with suffering and evil than an immanent one. If God is only transcendent, the question of why God allows suffering becomes unanswerable. It is only through an incarnational view that the tension can be resolved, and that is what the New Testament offers. The image of a suffering God who shares in human weakness and vulnerability may not be the kind of vision that inspires the building of grand empires. But it is the central biblical image, and the one that a Church for spiritual searchers most needs to recover.

Another urgent need is for **a renewed understanding of empowerment**. The Church's historic love affair with transcendence easily turns into a deep-seated unwillingness to allow – still less empower – those who are not the 'right' people to have any influence. This frequently expresses itself in a patriarchal form, as the contributions of women are marginalized and rejected, and overt images of maleness are continually projected as intrinsic to Christian faith – whether in the words of hymns, or the insistent use of exclusively male imagery for God.[51] The work of Russell Ackoff was critiqued in an earlier chapter, but for all its inadequacies and historical short-sightedness we can still learn from it. In his comparison of the Machine Age and the Systems Age, he observes that in the Machine Age

> employees were treated as replaceable machines or machine parts even though they were known to be human beings. Their personal objectives . . . were considered irrelevant by employers . . . the very simple repetitive tasks they were given to do were designed as though they were to be performed by machines.[52]

It is a sad fact that this description fits much church life too closely for comfort. There are hundreds of thousands of congregations where the members are only cogs in an ecclesiastical machine run by other people. More than that, there is no shortage of church leaders – especially at local level – who believe that is how it ought to be. But if people look at Christians and only see more of the destructive and disempowering systems that they struggle with in the rest of their lives, why should we expect them to be Christian? In describing the kind of environment in which people might flourish, Ackoff counsels that

> What is required is that individuals be able to evaluate their own quality of life, that they have an opportunity to improve it, that they be encouraged to do so, and that their efforts to do so be facilitated . . . [this will be brought about] by encouraging and facilitating the participation of the others in the design of and planning for the organizations and institutions of which they are a part.[53]

Now, where have we heard that before? Well how about starting with the New Testament – even, dare I say, with the life and example of Jesus? One of the major distinguishing marks of the way he called people into discipleship was his willingness to create the infrastructure of spirituality, not its superstructure. He then left his disciples to work out for themselves how and what to build on that infrastructure. Discipleship became their responsibility, not his, and facing that responsibility was, for them, a major component of what gave life its spiritual meaning.[54] That is the kind of context in which personal spiritual growth can take place.

A top-down style of being church rarely finds it possible to offer people effective solutions to their problems. For example, it is easy enough to *talk* about matters such as God's grace and forgiveness. But if the church only diagnoses the problems, without offering effective solutions, that is a very dangerous psychological and spiritual game. Moreover, as the rise of New Spirituality has demonstrated, people are increasingly looking for hands-on therapies. It simply will not do for solutions to be offered only in a theoretical sort of way. Knowing that there is an escape from guilt and failure is going to be of little practical assistance, if people then have to access it themselves without really knowing what is being recommended or required. Western people (the British perhaps more than most) love to keep themselves private. But leaving people to work out the implications of faith for themselves – just them and God in a secret place – can easily be understood as just another version of the destructive message that tells people they have only themselves to blame for their existential predicament. That is what has happened with those Calvinistic Christians mentioned earlier who regard themselves as unworthy to receive communion. There is no question that in a Reformed environment they will have heard verbal expositions of God's freely gifted grace and forgiveness, but because they are left high and dry with no idea of how to access that grace what sounds like (and ought to be) a liberating message becomes a prison for the soul. If the Holy Spirit offers the prospect of power to change – as the New Testament states clearly on every page – then the next question is, 'How do I access that power?' For that, rather more than theological statements will be required, however true they might be. There is a need for spiritual disciplines, techniques, and practices that will facilitate people in relating to their own inner selves, while consciously and deliberately opening their lives to God's presence, in order to effect radical change. There is also a need for a more playful spirituality.[55] Though it is often argued that the decline of the churches is related to their having become middle-class institutions, a more likely explanation is to be located in the inability of the church to appeal to those who have more intuitive and artistic ways of being. Paradoxically, there is a whole rich Christian tradition of interactive and affective (essentially non-cognitive) spirituality which had been marginalized and largely ignored until New Spirituality came along and began to ransack it. People need something tangible through which to express their deepest life commitments. But in order to explore them effectively, they need safe spaces. The creation of such spaces should be a top priority for the church – not only because it will assist the contextualization of the gospel in contemporary culture, but also because it is a way of being that is quite fundamental and central to the teaching of the New Testament.

Witness and service

Finally, we need to rediscover church as a focus for witness and service. Church is overwhelmingly perceived as either irrelevant or damaging. In some respects, this is part of a wider trend which we noticed in chapter 1, the tendency to mistrust institutions and to believe that they have all denied their original core values. All this would be bad enough by itself, but these are the very people who featured in David Hay's research as 'not going to church' but 'spiritual'.[56] Some of them have embarked on an intentional search for a meaningful spirituality that can offer trustworthy guidance to get them through life, while others appear to be having transcendent moments that they would identify as spiritual experiences, but with no reference points outside themselves whereby they can make sense of what has happened. So how can we refocus on gospel values in such a way that the church can begin to connect with people for whom it presently has no relevance, even – or especially – when they are spiritual searchers? This is a big question, and not one that can be addressed in the final paragraphs of this book. By way of excusing myself for not exploring it fully here, I will plead that I am in the process of writing another book that will face it head on, and will be the natural sequel to my earlier work *The McDonaldization of the Church*.[57] Two specific things can however be mentioned here, because they connect directly with the argument of the previous chapters: storytelling (which is about witness) and neighbourliness (which is about service). Lurking beneath these two, though, is a third fundamental issue, namely the question of leadership.

Recent years have seen a massive revival of **storytelling**, whether it be the grand narratives presented through the cinema or TV, or the homespun wisdom that is being shared in more informal, traditional storytelling networks that can range from major national and international festivals to a few friends getting together for a fireside chat. When I was a small boy, one of my favourite times of year was the Christmas holidays, and apart from getting time off school one of the things I looked forward to the most was gathering with older generations of my family, especially my grandparents, who would regale us with reminiscences of what life was like when they were children. To this day, I can still recall the names of some of their most notorious schoolteachers, and the incidents in which they were involved, even though none of it was within my own experience. If they were still alive today, researchers in oral history would be hot-footing it to their door to record their stories for posterity, because we have begun to appreciate that to have a meaningful sense of the self, we all need to see ourselves as part of a story that is bigger than our own lives. My grandparents and their stories – even though, in one sense, they concerned everyday trivialities – gave me a sense of who I was, where I had come from, and a confidence in who I might become. To a large extent, that sense of drawing meaning from the past has disappeared from Western culture, though it still survives in other parts of the world, and it is this loss that is driving the growing interest in storytelling. When the metanarratives that once guided our culture are no longer believed, we do not stop believing in metanarratives: we look for new ones. Philosopher François Lyotard famously declared that post-modernity involves 'incredulity toward metanarratives'[58] and most Christian commentators have assumed he was right, because of the way that the metanarrative inherited from a Christian past appears to have been abandoned as the basis of Western civilization.[59] But it is not that simple. For one thing, it is not so much the Christian metanarrative that has been abandoned, as the metanarrative of Christendom. In addition, what we now say we believe as a culture is so obviously dominated by metanarratives of one sort or another that one hardly needs to argue the case. How else can we characterize concepts of human rights, of globalization, of westernization, and McDonaldization – except as metanarratives? Moreover, we are every bit as insistent on imposing these grand stories on the rest of the world as our forebears were in the era of Christendom – and often with similarly damaging consequences. In terms of the personal spiritual search, the suspicion of metanarratives is not focused on the genre per se: what we are rejecting are those metanarratives that are damaging and disempowering. This no doubt also helps to explain why atheism is having such a hard time today, for the secular story emanating from rationalist-materialist thinking has also turned out to be damaging, to the planet as well as to persons. Antony Flew, a life-long atheist and philosophy professor, announced in autumn 2004 that he had changed his mind, albeit in a hesitating and somewhat unclear way.[60] He is certainly not alone in having second thoughts, and after a century or more in the ascendancy it is atheism that is now on the back foot.[61] We now live not only in a post-Christendom culture, but one that is also post-secular. There is a growing recognition that we are indeed spiritual beings, in all the multifarious ways identified in previous chapters of this book. This should be good news for Christians, though we cannot automatically assume that this spiritual interest will translate into following Jesus. In chapter 1, I highlighted the almost apocalyptic nature of our present plight, and it is no exaggeration to claim that the metanarrative that offers the best prospect of hope and meaning in a culture that is increasingly aware of its own lostness will be the one that shapes the future, not only of the West but (through the inevitable progress of globalization) the world. Christians sometimes take comfort from the fact that the Church is growing through much of the non-western world, and that is of course something to be aware of. But the idea that this will eventually work in reverse, and the West will be re-evangelized by that route, is almost certainly wishful thinking. We may not like it (and there are many reasons not to), but this is not how the future will be determined, especially not in a post 9/11 world that has seen the rise of a new imperialism among Western powers.

As a Christian, I have no doubt that the story of Jesus is the best hope for our world. But it is largely unheard in Western culture, and if I am right in thinking that what happens in the West will determine what happens in the rest of the world, that places much of the onus for effective evangelization back on Western Christians. In Western culture, the stories of Christendom and of the Church, and all the mistakes of the past, are well enough known and frequently retold. But the central core of the gospel as expressed by Jesus was the simple call to 'Follow me' (Matthew 8:22, 9:9, 10:38, 16:24, 19:21, and repeatedly in all the other Gospels). In order to follow faithfully in today's world, there will have to be a recognition of the mistakes of previous generations, and as part of that there will need to be appropriate expressions of repentance, even if in a technical sense we are not the ones who were most directly responsible. But over and above all that, we need a faithful telling of the story. As part of doing this, we will need to learn to trust God more. After all, if we do truly believe that God is active in this world (the *missio Dei*) and if we also regard people as 'made in God's image' (Genesis 1:27), and that the story of Jesus is a key bridge between the two, then there is a sense in which we can leave the outcome to God. And if we do not believe these things, then why is it worth being a Christian in the first place? This is not a blind fatalism in mission that just waits for things to happen, but an invitation to intentional waiting. When the prodigal son left home and departed for the far country, his father had every confidence that he would return. He did not try to cajole or bully the wayward son, but prepared the home for the day when he would return (Luke 15:11-32). It was an expectant and intentional waiting and preparation. Taking that story as some sort of model for mission with spiritual searchers, it invites Christians to be serious about central aspects of discipleship, such as faith, hope, trust, and prayer. But it also invites us to renew the furnishings in the home so that those who come find it a more life-giving environment than the pigsty. The starting point for that refurbishment will involve

Christians in hearing afresh for themselves the story of Jesus in all its radical challenge, and being prepared to do something about it.

One of the reasons that people find Jesus so attractive is that his message is not only one of personal empowerment, but also highlights the importance of **neighbourliness**. In reflecting on the significance of the insights offered by neurotheology, attention was drawn to the holistic nature of Jesus' call to discipleship as involving 'heart, soul, mind and strength' (a reference to the ancient Jewish prayer, the *Shema*). But he also went on to quote from another passage in the Hebrew scriptures, exhorting his followers to 'love your neighbour as yourself' (Mark 12:29-31). Christians have often ignored the intrinsic connection between these two aspects of Jesus' message, and have tended to emphasize doing good to others over and above personal development. The research of Heelas and Woodhead concluded that churches that do this ('congregations of humanity' in their terminology) have an even more uncertain future than other types of church.[67] In terms of gospel values, churches that are only social service organizations do not deserve to have a spiritual future – any more than do those that are exclusively focused on the internal, subjective concerns of individuals. Jesus is clear that the people who can make a difference in the world need to be at peace with themselves. Angry and fragmented people create an angry and fragmented world, while those who are whole spread peace and harmony. It is not an exegetical coincidence that these two statements are brought together: personal transformation and social concern are two sides of the same coin. The gospel declares that neither of them can be attained without a spiritual connection to God.

Both these aspects of Jesus' teaching reflect widely held convictions among people in general, whether or not they are self-consciously Christian. The important book by Jeremy Carrette and Richard King lays considerable emphasis on this. Indeed, one of their major complaints about what they regard as the commercial exploitation of the spiritual is that by focusing on the individual's inner life popular spiritualities are 'perpetuating a form of ethical myopia that turns our attention away from social injustice',[63] something they regard as entirely reprehensible because 'They promote accommodation to the social, economic and political mores of the day and provide little in terms of a challenge to the status quo or to a lifestyle of self-interest and ubiquitous consumption.'[64] Unfortunately, within the world view which they espouse, it is difficult to see why any of this should be regarded as a bad thing. Though they eventually conclude that 'it is the religions themselves that provide the best hope for humanity in challenging the God of Money',[65] religions are able to challenge such things because they tend to have a view on 'truth and authenticity' – a concern which Carrette and King dismiss at the very outset of their investigation as 'a misleading emphasis'.[66] I understand their desire to examine this field in as dispassionate a way as possible, so as to engage as wide a readership as they can. But some questions can only be addressed from a theological standpoint that invokes concepts such as justice and truth. Otherwise, given the universal tendency of people to exploit one another, what is to stop us behaving that way? Why not simply conclude that this is what people do, and accept it as being as natural a part of life as, say, drinking water, eating food, or having sex? At the same time, most people do seem to feel intuitively that dealing in devious and deceitful ways with others is wrong, even if they cannot quite put their finger on why they feel that way. The Christian explanation goes back to a theological tap root that will by now be very familiar to readers of this book: we are all made in God's image, and this by itself gives access to some understanding of how things are supposed to be. Unfortunately, Christians themselves often seem to forget that, which is why we end up projecting that judgemental image that dominates many people's impression of what Church is all about. A more appropriately prophetic way of proceeding was identified by Raymond Fung's presentation of *The Isaiah Vision*, in which he called for a renewed and faithful Church to begin with the recognition that we can only effectively challenge others to follow the way of Christ if we are continually hearing God's voice for ourselves, and allowing our own understandings to be changed in the process.[67] We have something to share with others not because we are different, but because we are no different, and we can become credible witnesses not as we condemn others and dismiss what we regard as their inadequate spiritualities, but as we constantly listen to the gospel and appropriate its challenge in our own lives. 'God leaves us free to choose how to share our faith. But our options are never neutral – every methodology either illustrates or betrays the gospel we announce'.[68] History offers many examples of Christians who have done that, and who made a significant contribution to the spread of gospel values in the wider culture, as well as the growth of the Church. It also reminds us that this is likely to be a costly and risky business, for those who are most admired are also often most marginalized. Dietrich Bonhoeffer, Martin Luther King, and Mother Teresa are but three names that spring immediately to mind in this connection, but for every one we know about there are thousands more whose faithful lives (and deaths) pass almost unnoticed.[69] For people who are serious about the spiritual search, what the Church offers can sometimes appear to be not only disconnected from real life, but also insufficiently challenging. In terms of effective mission, a delicate balance needs to be struck here. The Christian message is unlikely to be heard at all unless we are prepared to start where people are. But a fully Christian spirituality must always be prophetic and challenging, as well as personally fulfilling and redemptive. There has been much talk in recent years of evangelicals becoming more socially aware, and of more liberal Christians emphasizing personal transformation. But in many respects, the old demarcations still exist: in their Kendal Report, Heelas and Woodhead were able to draw a clear distinction between those churches with a social agenda and others with a more person-centred message, without feeling any need to justify it. Though they predicted a more promising future for evangelicals (especially charismatics), the basis for that judgement is precisely because such churches emphasize the private and personal dimensions of faith over and above concern for wider social and international issues.[70] Though I have not carried out the same sort of rigorous research as they did, that impression is certainly confirmed by my own experience. The worship of such churches is increasingly person-centred to the virtual exclusion of any wider vision, with a high dependence on introspective songs as being the heart of worship, and a corresponding lack of interest in issues wider than the individual's own self-awareness. In very many cases that I have personally seen, the world beyond the church might as well not exist, with even the perfunctory offering of intercessory prayer being relegated to a back seat, or excluded entirely. In such circumstances, worship might require higher energy levels than the sort of experience reported by Lee Pelham Cotton in the story with which this chapter began, but there can easily be the same level of disconnection between what passes as 'worship' and the issues that concern life beyond the four walls of church buildings. When church becomes a refuge from the rest of the world, some fundamental aspects of the gospel have been lost.

Finally, **leadership**. This is a big issue wherever we look in the Western world. Our entire culture has an ambivalent love-hate relationship with its leaders. On the one hand, we want leaders to know what they are doing, to be experts if you like, but at the same time we are resistant to accepting or trusting their expert opinion. Churches are not immune from this syndrome, and those with a Presbyterian or congregational type structure where everything is decided by committees seem almost to invite it. Whatever the historical justification for this way of being, the reality is that it no longer works as a leadership style in today's fast-changing world. Nor does it really deliver on its original theological promise of offering an inclusive way of being in which many people have an equal part. Committees are not accessible to everyone, but only to those who like committees and find themselves temperamentally attuned to that way of doing things. Moreover, even the spiritually sensitive committee can find its recommendations overturned by one or two people who throw their weight around. What we need today are people of vision and energy, who can see the needs and the opportunities, whose judgement will be trusted by others, but who in turn will be aware of their weaknesses as well as their strengths. Who those others might be is also relevant to mission with spiritual searchers. I recently visited a thriving church that had been started more or less from nothing (though at the initiative of a mainstream denomination), and among a group of people who by any definition would qualify as being spiritual searchers.

I was interested to learn that it began with a publicity drive aimed at those who were intentionally looking for spiritual ways of living, inviting such people to get in touch through either a phone number or an email address. Something like forty people had responded to this publicity (which was distributed through health clubs and other local outlets as well as through email to friends of friends). When they all got together, a core group of ten people was appointed to work out what they wanted to do, and how they would do it, and then report back to the larger group. Within little more than a year, the group had grown to more than a hundred people, all of them in their twenties, thirties, and forties, and eager for spiritual discoveries – and, as far as I could tell, faithfully exploring the gospel in relation to their lives. When I asked about the secret of their success, they were unequivocal in their response: that it was largely due to the fact that the core group of ten included non-Christians as well as Christians. From what I could gather, those who called themselves non-Christians had pushed the agenda forward faster and in more committed directions than the Christians who first initiated the group might have been inclined to do. The adoption of this model of 'power alongside' rather than 'power over' might sound risky, but in fact it is well grounded both theologically and in practice. It took seriously the belief that people, as people, are made in God's image. It also trusted God, not merely as a disembodied object of belief but as being active in the world and in people's lives (the *missio Dei* is more than just a theoretical construct). In the process, it created a safe space where people felt happy to bring their friends, knowing that they would be valued as persons, and their life experience would be taken seriously. It is so simple that I wonder why I am writing about it – except I know the answer to that, for it challenges the tendency to conformity and control that is deeply embedded in most existing church structures. In doing so, however, it recognizes the validity of Jesus' advice that 'those who are not against us are for us' (Mark 9:40). In the process, it also embodies the leadership style of Jesus, eloquently (and accurately) described in the words of management consultant Laurie Beth Jones: 'He did not brand them. He did not hand them maps, or whips, or chains, or even time cards. He gave them a new breath of the spirit that is Holy, and they were never the same.'[71]

This final chapter has merely scratched the surface of what Christians now need to be and do in order to bear effective witness to the gospel in an ever-changing but increasingly spiritual culture. A lot more could be said, and will be in my next book. For some, my approach will seem too woolly and open-ended. I will not be surprised if others dismiss it as even dangerous. But mission is always both costly and risky, and we live in risky times. The entire fabric of Western civilization is being rewoven in our lifetime, and the future of the world will be determined by the threads that go to make up the new cloth. The Church in the West is faced with hard choices. To do nothing is not an option: all the indicators point to near-extinction, and even those who are committed to the Church find themselves increasingly pessimistic in their projections for the future. We therefore have everything to play for. The very worst that can happen is that every risky step we take turns out to be wrong – in which case the Church ends up in a mess, but no greater a mess than is likely if we refuse to take the risk. On the other hand – because I believe not only in taking risks, but also in God – we might just find ourselves for once working in harmony with the *missio Dei*, in ways that will breathe new life not only into the Church but into the wider culture. This book is written for those who are prepared to take the risk. It will not be the last word, but I believe that the approach offered here holds out new possibilities of personal healing and wholeness in a fragmented world, as well as the prospect of a Church renewed in its own soul. Actually (and here is a final theological point), its very weakness is likely to be the secret of its power, and in that respect it will be incarnational in every sense of the word, for this is how Jesus himself came bearing the good news. And even St Paul – often unfairly castigated as a revisionist commentator on the message of Jesus – reminded his readers in Corinth (who, of all people, were tempted to think that they could best do God's work in their own way and by their own power) that 'God chose what is foolish in the world to shame the wise; God chose what is weak in the world to shame the strong; God chose what is low and despised in the world, things that are not, to reduce to nothing things that are . . .' (1

Corinthians 1:27-8). In our struggle to find new ways of being church in a context of rapid cultural change, that is perhaps the best news of all, and the most truly empowering message for the people of a post-modern age who are searching for spiritual meaning.

Notes

Preface

1. *The Collected Poems of W.B. Yeats* (London: Macmillan, 1961), 81. Originally published in the collection *The Wind Among the Reeds* (1899).

Chapter 1: From 'Religion' to 'Spirituality'

1. *The Whole Person*, August 2004 (Santa Barbara: Whole Person, 2004), 7.
2. The Rider-Waite Tarot Pack which he created is still regarded as the definitive version: cf. John Drane, Ross Clifford and Philip Johnson, *Beyond Prediction: the Tarot and your Spirituality* (Oxford: Lion, 2001).
3. Steve Bruce, *Religion in Modern Britain* (Oxford: Oxford University Press, 1995), 95-124; *God is Dead: secularization in the West* (Oxford: Blackwell, 2002), 75-105.
4. Paul Heelas, *The New Age Movement: the celebration of the self and the sacralization of modernity* (Oxford: Blackwell, 1996).
5. Jeremy Carrette and Richard King, *Selling Spirituality: the silent takeover of religion* (London: Routledge, 2004), 1.
6. See Walter Truett Anderson, *The Next Enlightenment* (New York: St Martin's Press, 2003). The phrases quoted are on pages 179, 180.
7. Denise Cush, 'British Buddhism and the New Age' in *Journal of Contemporary Religion* 11/2 (1996), 196.
8. Marilyn Ferguson, *The Aquarian Conspiracy* (London: Paladin, 1982), 30.
9. Carol Riddell, *The Findhorn Community* (Findhorn: Findhorn Press, 1990), 64. The Findhorn Foundation and Community is one of the world's most influential centres for New Spirituality. Located in north-east Scotland, it is home to a permanent community of about 400 people, but has thousands of visitors from all over the world who go to experience its unique blend of spiritual traditions: visit www.findhorn.org. For a further account of some aspects of its life, see Stephen J. Sutcliffe, *Children of the New Age* (London: Routledge, 2003), 150-73.
10. I am using the term 'spiritual searcher' here in the technical sense proposed in my book *The McDonaldization of the Church* (London: Darton, Longman & Todd, 2000), 69-73.
11. Cf. John Drane, *What is the New Age still saying to the Church* (London: HarperCollins, 1999).
12. For an excellent historical survey of the use of the term 'spirituality' see Carrette and King, *Selling Spirituality*, 30-53.
13. *ibid.*, 1-29.

14. R. Fuller, *Spiritual but not Religious: Understanding Unchurched America* (New York: Oxford University Press, 2001).
15. Rodney Clapp, *Tortured Wonders: Christian Spirituality for people, not angels* (Grand Rapids: Brazos, 2004), 11.
16. *ibid.*, 12.
17. James Gollnick, 'Religion, Spirituality and Implicit Religion in Psychotherapy', in *Implicit Religion* 7/2 (2004), 120-41.
18. Popularized by the *Left Behind* series, authored by Tim LaHaye and Jerry B. Jenkins, published by Tyndale House Publishers, and now extending to more than a dozen volumes, as well as a series of movies.
19. George Lings, *Living Proof - a new way of being church?* (Sheffield: Church Army, 1999), 13-14.
20. For an introduction to the use of this term in social science research, see George Ritzer, *McDonaldization: the Reader* (Thousand Oaks: Pine Forge Press, 2002); and for its application to the Church, see Drane, *The McDonaldization of the Church.*
21. While the impetus behind the emergence of the New Spirituality is directly related to problems within the inherited Western world view, this does not mean that it is an exclusively Western phenomenon. Precisely because of its underlying rationale, it tends to regard other world views as sources of spiritual wisdom, and as well as paying attention to the insights of various ancient civilizations long since disappeared it also values traditional understandings found in the living cultures of non-western countries. At the same time, this is not a one-way exchange of ideas, and because of the rapid globalization (which is in fact the Westernization) of the world community, there is a more immediate transfer of ideas between cultures than has ever been the case in previous generations, and this is leading to the growing worldwide popularity of the same kind of New Spirituality that is most evident in the West.
22. Friedrich Nietzsche, *The Joyful Wisdom*, Book 3, section 108; originally in German 1882, English translation by Thomas Common, vol. 10 of *The Complete Works of Friedrich Nietzsche* (Edinburgh: T.N. Foulis, 1910), 151.
23. Steve Bruce, *God is Dead: Secularization in the West* (Oxford: Blackwell, 2002).
24. Peter Brierley, *The Tide is Running Out* (London: Christian Research, 2000), 236.
25. This figure compares with 15.1% who claimed to be 'of no religion', 2.8% who are Muslim, with a further 2.6% accounting for all other major religious groupings put together (Judaism, Hinduism, Buddhism, and others). 7.8% of respondents did not answer this question on the census forms (response was voluntary). See http://www.statistics.gov.uk/cci/nugget.asp?id=954.
26. Cf. Leslie J. Francis, 'Religion and Social Capital: the flaw in the 2001 census in England and Wales', in Paul Avis (ed.), *Public Faith* (London: SPCK, 2003), 45-64.

27. Callum Brown, *The Death of Christian Britain* (London: Routledge, 2000), 198.
28. Harvey Cox, 'The Myth of the Twentieth Century: the rise and fall of "secularization"', in Gregory Baum (ed.), *The Twentieth Century: a Theological Overview* (Maryknoll: Orbis, 1999), 136. Cf. also Peter L. Berger (ed.), *The Desecularization of the World* (Grand Rapids: Eerdmans, 1999).
29. Paul Heelas and Linda Woodhead, *The Spiritual Revolution* (Oxford: Blackwell, 2005); see also the website www.kendalproject.org.uk.
30. Heelas and Woodhead, *Spiritual Revolution*, 136.
31. *ibid.*, 137.
32. Brierley, *The Tide is Running Out*, 28.
33. Michel de Certeau, *The Practice of Everyday Life* (Berkeley: University of California Press, 1984), 70.
34. B. Joseph Pine and James H. Gilmore, *The Experience Economy* (Boston: Harvard Business School, 1999), 163-4, 183.
35. Cf. A. Maslow, *Motivation and Personality* (New York: Harper & Row, 1954), *Toward a Psychology of Being* (New York: Van Nostrand, 1962); Frederick S. Perls, Ralph F. Hefferline and Paul Goodman, *Gestalt Therapy: excitement and growth in the human personality* (New York: Julian Press, 1951); Frederick S. Perls, *In and out the garbage pail* (Lafayette CA: Real People Press, 1969); Willard B. Frick (ed.), *Humanistic psychology: interviews with Maslow, Murphy, and Rogers* (Columbus OH: Merrill, 1971); Carl R. Rogers, *Becoming a person: Part 1. Some hypotheses regarding the facilitation of personal growth; Part 2. What it means to become a person* (Oberlin OH: Oberlin College, 1954).
36. The Nag Hammadi Library, consisting of thirteen ancient codices containing over fifty separate texts, was discovered in upper Egypt in 1945 and appears to have been collected late in the third century AD and during the fourth. Soon after their discovery, some of the documents were sold on the black market, and what is now known as Codex I was bought for the C.G. Jung Institute in Zurich, hence its name 'The Jung Codex'. Among other texts, it contains *The Gospel of Truth* and *The Treatise on the Resurrection*. There are various published editions of all the texts, but for an accessible (and scholarly) account, see www.gnosis.org.
37. Martin Rees, *Our Final Century* (London: Heinemann, 2003), 8.
38. On cultural change as a catalyst, see Lorne L. Dawson, *Comprehending Cults: the sociology of New Religious Movements* (Toronto: Oxford University Press, 1998), 42-62.
39. Douglas Coupland, *Life after God* (New York: Simon & Schuster, 1994). The quotations are taken from the front dust jacket of the Pocketbooks edition.
40. *ibid.*, 359.
41. Within the realm of theological study, this is an emerging discipline, the shape of which is still much debated. For introductions offering an overview, see Ray S. Anderson, *The Shape of Practical Theology* (Downers Grove: InterVarsity, 2001); Paul Ballard and John Pritchard, *Practical theol-*

ogy in action: Christian thinking in the service of church and society (London: SPCK, 1996); Don Browning, *A fundamental practical theology: descriptive and strategic proposals* (Minneapolis: Fortress Press, 1991); James Woodward and Stephen Pattison (eds.), *The Blackwell Reader in Pastoral and Practical Theology* (Oxford: Blackwell, 1999).

42. Truett Anderson, *Next Enlightenment*, 9.
43. Cf. John Drane, 'From Creeds to Burgers: religious control, spiritual search, and the future of the world', in James R. Beckford and John Walliss, *Religion and Social Theory* (London: Ashgate, forthcoming 2005); also in George Ritzer, *McDonaldization: the Reader*, 2nd edn (Thousand Oaks: Sage, forthcoming 2005).
44. Charles Lyell, *Principles of Geology* (London: John Murray, 1830–3).
45. The final sentence of chapter XIV, Recapitulation and Conclusion. For a recent edition, see Charles Darwin, *The Origin of Species* (Ware: Wordsworth Classics, 1998), 369.
46. Charles Dickens, *A Tale of Two Cities* (1859), Book 2:VII.
47. Carl A. Raschke, *The Interruption of Eternity: Modern Gnosticism and the Origins of the New Religious Consciousness* (Chicago: Nelson-Hall, 1980), 42.
48. On all this see, e.g., James E. Talmage, *A Study of the Articles of Faith* (London: Church of Jesus Christ of Latter Day Saints, 1962); quote is from Parley P. Pratt, *Key to the Science of Theology* (Salt Lake City: Deseret Books, 1973 reprint), 40-1 (see the entire section 34-81).
49. See J.N. Darby, *Synopsis of the books of the Bible*, 2nd edn (New York: Loizeaux Brothers, 1950), originally published 1857–64; C.I. Scofield, *The Scofield Reference Bible* (London: Oxford University Press, 1909).
50. See Edmund W. Gosse, *Father and Son* (London: Heinemann, 1907).
51. Cf. among many others Timothy Leary, *Turn on, Tune in, Drop out* (Berkeley: Ronin Publishing, 1999); *Your Brain is God* (Berkeley: Ronin Publishing, 2001).
52. Alan Watts, *The Book: on the Taboo against knowing who you are* (New York: Vintage, 1982).
53. *ibid.*, 12.
54. Cf. Rollo May, *The Courage to Create* (New York: W.W. Norton, 1975); Carl R. Rogers, *Client-Centered Therapy* (London: Constable, 1951).
55. Cf. James Gollnick, 'Religion, Spirituality, and Implicit Religion in Psychotherapy', in *Implicit Religion* 7/2 (2004), 120-41.
56. Fritjof Capra, *The Tao of Physics* (London: Fontana, 1976).
57. Fritjof Capra, *The Turning Point* (London: Flamingo, 1983), xvii.
58. Niels Bohr, *Atomic Physics and Human Knowledge* (New York: John Wiley, 1958), 20.
59. Ferguson, *The Aquarian Conspiracy*, 30.
60. 'The members speak: what does "New Age" mean to you?', *New Age Journal* (November–December 1987), 52.
61. J.L. Simmons, *The Emerging New Age* (Santa Fe: Bear & Co., 1990), 83.

62. Robert S. Elwood, *Islands of the Dawn: the story of alternative spirituality in New Zealand* (Honolulu: University of Hawaii Press, 1993), 246.
63. Carrette and King, *Selling Spirituality*, 49.
64. *ibid.*, 77.
65. *ibid.*, 125.
66. Starhawk, *The Spiral Dance* (San Francisco: Harper & Row, 1989), 214.
67. Ziauddin Sardar, *Postmodernism and the Other* (London: Pluto Press, 1998), quotations from pages 225 and 13. Of course, Western people are not the only ones who raid other cultures indiscriminately, taking what they find appealing and leaving the rest: non-western governments are doing it all the time, as they want to be included in the world family of nations and to share in the prosperity generated by world trade, but are less inclined to take on board values such as human rights or democracy.
68. Carrette and King, *Selling Spirituality*, 15.
69. *ibid.*, 132.
70. *ibid.*, 3; their original italics.
71. *ibid.*, 68.
72. Alan Jamieson, *A Churchless Faith: Faith journeys beyond the Churches* (London: SPCK, 2002). Also William D. Hendricks, *Exit Interviews* (Chicago: Moody Press, 1993); Philip J. Richter and Leslie J. Francis, *Gone but not Forgotten: Church leaving and returning* (London: Darton, Longman & Todd, 1998). For a personal story, see Gordon Lynch, *Losing my Religion?* (London: Darton, Longman & Todd, 2003).

Chapter 2: Spirituality in Everyday Life

1. Stephen Pattison, in H. Orchard (ed.), *Spirituality in Healthcare Contexts* (London: Jessica Kingsley, 2001), 37.
2. Jeremy Carrette and Richard King, *Selling Spirituality* (London: Routledge, 2004), 125.
3. Donald W. McCormick, 'Spirituality and Management', in *Journal of Managerial Psychology* 9/6 (1994), 5.
4. Rodney Clapp, *Tortured Wonders* (Grand Rapids: Brazos Press, 2004), 13.
5. L. Wittgenstein, *Philosophical Investigations* (Oxford: Blackwell, 1968), sections 65-78.
6. Elliott Miller, *A Crash Course on the New Age Movement* (Grand Rapids: Baker, 1989), 14.
7. Cf. Marilyn Ferguson, *The Aquarian Conspiracy* (London: Paladin, 1982), 231-41; Michael York, *The Emerging Network* (Lanham MD: Rowman & Littlefield, 1995), 324-34; Michael York, 'The New Age in Britain Today', *Religion Today* 9/3 (1994), 14-21.
8. Donal Dorr, *Time for a Change* (Dublin: Columba Press, 2004), 37.
9. For examples of 'spirituality' in the business world, cf. Lee G. Bolman and Terence E. Deal, *Leading with Soul: an uncommon journey of spirit* (San Francisco: Jossey-Bass, 2001); Catherine McGeachy, *Spiritual Intelligence in*

the Workplace (Dublin: Veritas, 2001); Antonia Swinson, *Root of all Evil? Making spiritual values count* (Edinburgh: St Andrew Press, 2003).

10. Russell Ackoff, *Creating the Corporate Future* (New York: Wiley, 1981); on systems theory cf. L. von Bertalanffy, *General System Theory* (New York: George Brazillier, 1968); *Perspectives on General System Theory* (New York: George Brazillier, 1975).
11. James Lovelock, *Gaia: a new look at life on earth* (Oxford: Oxford University Press, 1979).
12. For an interpretation of these trends consistent with New Spirituality, written by a scientist, see Fritjof Capra, *The Web of Life* (London: Flamingo, 1997).
13. Ackoff, *Creating the Corporate Future*, 25-6.
14. *ibid.*, 19-20.
15. *ibid.*, 19.
16. *ibid.*, 13.
17. Jose Arguelles, 'Harmonic Convergence, Trigger event: implementation and follow-up', in *Life Times Magazine* 3 (1987), 65.
18. In an interview with the *Chicago Tribune* (25 May 1916).
19. Ackoff, *Creating the Corporate Future*, 25.
20. For a vigorous argument along these lines, see Matthew Fox, *The Reinvention of Work* (San Francisco: HarperSanFrancisco, 1994); also Robert Banks, *God the Worker* (Valley Forge: Judson Press, 1994).
21. In a survey of over 100 managers, based on in-depth interviews, Ian I. Mitroff and Elizabeth A. Denton discovered that more than 90% of them had a positive view of 'spirituality' in relation to daily work: see their article 'A study of spirituality in the workplace' in *Sloan Management Review* 40/4 (1999), 83-92.
22. Barrie Dolnick, *The Executive Mystic* (New York: HarperBusiness, 1998).
23. *ibid.*, xvi-xvii.
24. *ibid.*, xvii.
25. *ibid.*, xviii, 31.
26. *ibid.*, 154.
27. Walter Truett Anderson, *The Next Enlightenment* (New York: St Martin's Press, 2003), 183-4.
28. Dolnick, *The Executive Mystic*, 146.
29. *ibid.*, 10.
30. *ibid.*, 121-4.
31. *ibid.*, 11.
32. *ibid.*, 37.
33. For all these things, see *ibid.*, 33-63.
34. *ibid.*, 203-26.
35. *ibid.*, 94.
36. *ibid.*, 105.
37. For these, and other examples, see *ibid.*, 173-4.
38. *ibid.*, 10.

39. *A Course in Miracles* (New York: Foundation for Inner Peace, 1975).
40. On the spiritual consequences of this, see John Drane, *The McDonaldization of the Church* (London: Darton, Longman & Todd, 2000), 73-5.
41. Sharon Janis, *Spirituality for Dummies* (New York: Hungry Minds, 2000).
42. For this biographical information, see www.kumuda.com.
43. Janis, *Spirituality for Dummies*, 17.
44. *ibid.*, 10.
45. Joycelin Dawes, Janice Dolley, and Ike Isaksen, *The Quest: Exploring a sense of Soul* (Ropley: O Books, 2005).
46. C. Diane Ealy, *The Complete Idiot's Guide to Spirituality in the Workplace* (Indianapolis: Alpha Books, 2002).
47. *ibid.*, 16.
48. *ibid.*, 130.
49. Linda Woodhead, 'The turn to life in contemporary religion and spirituality', in Ursula King (ed.), *Spirituality and Society in the New Millennium* (Brighton: Sussex Academic Press, 2001), 110-23.
50. Paul Heelas and Linda Woodhead, *The Spiritual Revolution* (London: Routledge, 2005), 2.
51. Don Cupitt, *The New Religion of Life in Everyday Speech* (London: SCM, 1999).
52. On this, see John Drane, *Cultural Change and Biblical Faith* (Carlisle: Paternoster Press, 2000), 78-103.
53. Cupitt, *New Religion of Life*, 2.
54. *ibid.*, 89-96.
55. *ibid.*, Foreword.
56. *ibid.*, 90.
57. *ibid.*, 13.
58. *ibid.*, 53-64.
59. *ibid.*, 97.
60. *ibid.*, 9.
61. *ibid.*, 96-7.
62. Abraham Maslow, *Motivation and Personality*, 2nd edn (New York: Harper & Row, 1970).
63. Rick Warren, *The Purpose Driven Life* (Grand Rapids: Zondervan, 2003).
64. Nicky Gumbel, *Alpha: Questions of Life* (Eastbourne: Kingsway, 2003); see also Nicky Gumbel, *A Life Worth Living* (Eastbourne: Kingsway, 2001), *Challenging Lifestyle: exploring the meaning of Life* (Eastbourne: Kingsway, 2001).
65. See for example Ray S. Anderson, *Spiritual Caregiving as Secular Sacrament* (London: Jessica Kingsley, 2003); Norman Drummond, *The Spirit of Success: how to connect your heart to your head in work and life* (London: Hodder, 2004) – both of them good examples of how it is possible to connect Christian values and lifestyle spirituality in a creative way.
66. Stephen Hunt, *The Alpha Enterprise* (London: Ashgate, 2004), 45.

67. Heelas and Woodhead, *Spiritual Revolution*, 147.
68. Cf. Pete Ward, *Selling Worship: how what we sing has changed the Church* (Carlisle: Paternoster Press, 2005).
69. Cf. John Drane, *The McDonaldization of the Church;* and 'From Creeds to Burgers: religious control, spiritual search, and the future of the world', in James R. Beckford and John Walliss, *Religion and Social Theory* (London: Ashgate, forthcoming 2005); also in George Ritzer, *McDonaldization: the Reader*, 2nd edn (Thousand Oaks: Sage, forthcoming 2005).
70. For an informed account of neo-paganism, see Graham Harvey, *Listening People, Speaking Earth: Contemporary Paganism* (London: Hurst & Co., 1997). There is a good deal of debate as to whether this really is a rediscovery of the past, or whether it is not an imposition on the past of a modern agenda. Cf. Ronald Hutton, 'Neo-Paganism, Paganism & Christianity', in *Religion Today* 9/3 (1994), 29-32. Also the discussions of the allegation that Christianity (= 'patriarchy') displaced an original goddess-centred matriarchal culture: Mary Jo Weaver, 'Who is the Goddess and Where does she get us?', in *Journal of Feminist Studies in Religion* 5/1 (1989), 49-64; Sally Binford, 'Are Goddesses and Matriarchies Merely Figments of Feminist Imagination?', in *The Politics of Women's Spirituality*, ed. Charlene Spretnak (Garden City NY: Doubleday, 1982), 541-9.
71. David Spangler and William Irwin Thomson, *Reimagination of the World* (Santa Fe: Bear & Co., 1991), xvi.
72. Carol Riddell, *The Findhorn Community* (Findhorn: Findhorn Press, 1990), 63, italics mine.
73. Heelas and Woodhead, *Spiritual Revolution*, 32.
74. The Pentecostal/Charismatic strand of world Christianity has grown from nothing at the start of the twentieth century to become a major force in the world Church. A common way of describing its history is to regard the first wave as the Pentecostal movement itself, which led to the emergence of Pentecostal denominations such as Assemblies of God and the International Church of the Foursquare Gospel, with the second wave comprising the charismatic movement of the 1960s and onwards, which led to the establishment of charismatic beliefs and practices in other mainline churches, both Catholic and Protestant. The so-called third wave came to be associated with the ministry of John Wimber and the Vineyard Christian Fellowship, and was specially characterized by 'signs and wonders' apparently demonstrating access to supernatural powers, including the Toronto Blessing which involved laughing and roaring 'in the Spirit' as a sign that God was reclaiming lost territory. See C. Peter Wagner, *The Third Wave of the Holy Spirit* (Ann Arbor: Vine Books, 1988); and for a more dispassionate account, David Hilborn (ed.), *Toronto in Perspective* (Carlisle: Paternoster Press, 2002).
75. William James, *The Varieties of Religious Experience* (New York: Longmans, Green & Co., 1902).
76. See especially C.G. Jung, *Modern Man in Search of a Soul* (London: Kegan

Paul, Trench, Trubner, 1933); and Robert Segal *The Gnostic Jung* (London: Routledge, 1992).

77. Alister Hardy, *The Living Stream* (Glasgow: Collins, 1965); also *The Biology of God: a Scientist's study of man the religious animal* (New York: Taplinger Publishing Co., 1976); *Spiritual Nature of Man: study of contemporary religious experience* (Oxford: Oxford University Press, 1979). For an appreciative assessment of Hardy's work, see David Hay, *Alister Hardy - Biologist of the Spirit* (Oxford: Religious Experience Research Centre, 1998).
78. Richard Bucke, *Cosmic Consciousness: a study in the evolution of the human mind* (New Hyde Park NY: University Books, 1961).
79. Peter Berger, *The Sacred Canopy: Elements of a Sociological Theory of Religion* (New York: Doubleday, 1967), 5.
80. Cf. Karl Barth, *Church Dogmatics* vol. 3, *The Doctrine of Creation, Part 1* (Edinburgh: T & T Clark, 1958).
81. Andrew Newberg and Eugene D'Aquili, *Why God won't go away*, 2nd edn (New York: Ballantine, 2002).
82. SPECT is an acronym for Single Photon Emission Computed Tomography, which is a high-tech imaging tool capable of detecting radioactive emissions. For details of the experiments, see *Why God won't go away*, 1-10.
83. Newberg and D'Aquili, *Why God won't go away*, 34.
84. *ibid.*, 36.
85. *ibid.*, 37.
86. *ibid.*, 146-7.
87. *ibid.*, 100.
88. *ibid.*, 108.
89. *ibid.*, 155.
90. David Hay and Kate Hunt, *Understanding the Spirituality of People who don't go to Church* (Nottingham: University of Nottingham Centre for the Study of Human Relations, 2000).
91. Dean Hamer, *The God Gene: how Faith is hardwired into our genes* (New York: Doubleday, 2004).
92. Cloninger is Wallace Renard Professor of Psychiatry and Genetics at Washington University School of Medicine. See C. Robert Cloninger, *Feeling Good: the science of wellbeing* (New York: Oxford University Press, 2004).
93. Rick Strassman, *DMT: the Spirit Molecule* (Rochester VT: Park Street Press, 2001).
94. *ibid.*, 62.
95. Autopsies on the brains of people who commit suicide invariably display a diminished level of serotonin, which many neuroscientists believe is a trigger for erratic and destructive behaviour even though wider social factors may also play a part. Cf. Carol Ezzell, 'The Neuroscience of Suicide', in *Scientific American* (February 2003), 33-9.
96. For an accessible account, see René Descartes, 'The inter-relation of soul

and body', in P. Wheelwright (ed.), *The Way of Philosophy* (New York: Odyssey, 1954), 357.

97. Strassman, *DMT: the Spirit Molecule*, 83. It probably goes without saying that not everyone agrees with the underlying assumption made here by Strassman, namely that personhood and personality is in some way intrinsically related to biology, whether through a genetic or chemical route. For a different view, arguing that personhood is actually a social construct, cf. Mario Moussa and Thomas Shannon, 'The Search for the New Pineal Gland: Brain Life and Personhood' in *Hastings Center Report* 22 (1992), 30-7.
98. Strassman, *DMT: the Spirit Molecule*, 61.
99. *ibid.*, 68-9.
100. Augustine, *Confessions*, Book I.1. For a modern translation, see *Augustine Confessions Books I-XIII*, translated by F.J. Sheed, Introduction by Peter Brown (Indianapolis: Hackett Publishing Co., 1993), 3.
101. Compare and contrast the perspectives offered by Warren S. Brown, Nancey Murphy, and H. Newton Malony (eds.), *Whatever happened to the Soul?: scientific and theological portraits of human nature* (Minneapolis: Fortress Press, 1998) with the discussions in Joel Green (ed.), *What about the Soul? Neuroscience and Christian Anthropology* (Nashville: Abingdon Press, 2004).
102. In the case of Newberg's approach, the answer might well be 'yes', because there is a good deal of evidence to show that when the discrete functions of one hemisphere of the brain are disabled, fresh neural pathways can open up in the other hemisphere. Cf. Sally P. Springer and Georg Deutsch, *Left Brain, Right Brain*, 4th edn (New York: W.H. Freeman & Co., 1993). Some recent research has shown that in people born blind, the parts of the brain that control touch expand to take over the neural capacity of those parts that normally involve vision, thus making it easier for them to operate with Braille than a sighted person would be able to do: cf. N. Sadato *et al.*, 'Neural Networks for Braille reading by the Blind' in *Brain* 121 (1998), 1213-29. On the basis of his genetic argument, it is worth noting that Hamer does not claim that a particular genetic combination guarantees that an individual will adopt an overtly 'spiritual' approach to life – only that they are likely to do so. Personal choice is therefore built into his approach, and arguably that in itself is part of a meaningful spiritual journey.
103. On this, cf. Michael Grimshaw, 'I can't believe my eyes: the religious aesthetics of sport as postmodern salvific moments', in *Implicit Religion* 3/2 (2000), 87-99; Shirl J. Hoffman, *Sport and Religion* (Champaign IL: Human Kinetics Books, 1992); Craig Detweiler and Barry Taylor, *A Matrix of Meanings* (Grand Rapids: Baker Academic, 2003), 243-69.
104. Cf. Christopher H. Evans and William R. Herzog, *The Faith of 50 Million: baseball, religion, and American culture* (Louisville: Westminster John Knox Press, 2002).

105. Strassman, *DMT: the Spirit Molecule*, 327.
106. Cf. Nicholas Goodrick-Clarke, *The Occult Roots of Nazism* (London: Tauris, 1992). It is also the case, however, that others who were inspired by the Western esoteric tradition opposed Hitler and were involved in a plot to overthrow him: see Michael Baigent and Richard Leigh, *Secret Germany: Stauffenberg and the Mystical Crusade against Hitler* (London: Penguin, 1995).
107. *World* for 26 February 2005. The full text of the article from which these quotations are derived was accessed on 8 March 2005 at http://www.worldmag.com/subscriber/displayarticle.cfm?id=10368.
108. In *Sightings* for 7 March 2005, a weekly email bulletin from the Martin Marty Center at the University of Chicago Divinity School.
109. Cf. the 'myth and ritual' school of S.H. Hooke, *et al.*, who – starting from a totally different premise – regarded ritual as the active outworking of the kind of archetypal images presented in 'myth'. J.G. Frazer, *The Golden Bough: a study in comparative religion* (London: Macmillan, 1890); S.H. Hooke, *Myth and Ritual* (London: Oxford University Press, 1933).
110. Newberg and D'Aquili, *Why God won't go away*, 91.
111. Starhawk, Th*e Spiral Dance* (San Francisco: Harper & Row, 1979), 214.
112. Walter Hooper (ed.), *God in the Dock* (London: Fount, 1979), 45.
113. Shirley Maclaine, *Out on a Limb* (London: Bantam, 1987), 215.
114. Newberg and D'Aquili, *Why God won't go away*, 96.

Chapter 3: New Spirituality and Christian Mission

1. Lawrence Osborn, 'The Gospel in the New Age', *Gospel and Culture* 18 (autumn 1993), 1-5. Paul Heelas and Linda Woodhead, *The Spiritual Revolution* (London: Routledge, 2005), 132, see this as a potential weakness in New Spirituality, and wonder if future generations brought up with no connection with church will be as interested in it as the baby boomer generation. But if I am correct in identifying the all-embracing breadth of the spiritual, it seems to me more likely that, while the configurations may change in the future, the underlying reality is unlikely to be diminished.
2. Cf. Paul Vallely, 'Evangelism in a Post-Religious Society', in *Setting the Agenda: the Report of the 1999 Church of England Conference on Evangelism* (London: Church House Publishing, 1999), 30-43.
3. For a basic introduction to his ideas, see his *Original Blessing* (Santa Fe: Bear & Co., 1983), and *Confessions* (San Francisco: HarperSanFrancisco, 1996).
4. For my own comments on Matthew Fox's methods and conclusions, see the article 'Matthew Fox', in Trevor Hart (ed.), *The Dictionary of Historical Theology* (Carlisle: Paternoster/Grand Rapids: Eerdmans, 2000), 218-20. Cf. also Richard Bauckham, 'The New Age Theology of Matthew Fox: a Christian theological response', in *Anvil* 13/2 (1996), 115-26.
5. Darren Kemp, *The Christaquarians: a Sociology of Christians in the New Age* (London: Kempress, 2003).
6. For examples of this approach, see Constance Cumbey, *The Hidden Dangers*

of the Rainbow (Lafayette LA: Huntington House, 1983); Alan Morrison, *The Serpent and the Cross* (Birmingham: K & M Books, 1994).

7. Cf. L.J. Francis and M.T. Stubbs, 'Measuring attitudes towards Christianity: from childhood into adulthood', in *Personality and Individual Differences* 8 (1987), 741-3; L.J. Francis, 'Psychological Type and Mystical Orientation', in *Pastoral Sciences* 21/1 (2002), 77-93; Leslie Francis, 'Personality Type and Communicating the Gospel', in *Modern Believing* 42/1 (2001), 32-46.
8. Satanists, like Christians, come in several different forms. The most significant group today is the Church of Satan, founded in the 1960s by Anton LaVey. He used the notion of 'Satan' to symbolize a way of life set free from cultural taboos and conventional restrictions, with no implied theological world view or basis to it. Cf. Gavin Baddeley, *Lucifer Rising: a Book of Sin, Devil Worship and Rock 'n' Roll* (London: Plexus, 1999); James R. Lewis, *Satanism Today: an encyclopedia of Religion, Folklore, and Popular Culture* (Santa Barbara: ABC-Clio, 2001); Graham Harvey, 'Satanism in Britain Today', in *Journal of Contemporary Religion* 10 (1995), 283-96.
9. Cf. movies such as *The Exorcist*, which has been remade in several versions since its original release in 1973; *The Omen*, which became the first of a series of four films on the same theme, beginning in 1976; and *Amityville Horror* (1979).
10. Irving Hexham, 'The Evangelical Response to the New Age', in J.R. Lewis and J.G. Melton, *Perspectives on the New Age* (Albany NY: SUNY Press, 1992), 152-63. Quotations are from pages 159 and 161.
11. Irving Hexham, Stephen Rost and John W. Morehead, *Encountering New Religious Movements: a Holistic Evangelical Approach* (Grand Rapids: Kregel, 2004).
12. *ibid.*, 211-12.
13. *ibid.*, 201.
14. The same comment could be made of the propensity of some Christians to see New Spirituality as essentially an occult movement. While some traditionally occult practices are undoubtedly followed by some spiritual searchers, this is a tiny proportion of the entire movement (I would estimate that less than 10% of it falls into this category). Cf. B.J. Gibbons, *Spirituality and the Occult from the renaissance to the modern age* (London: Routledge, 2001).
15. Cf. Rudolf Bultmann, *History and Eschatology* (Edinburgh: Edinburgh University Press, 1957); *Jesus Christ and Mythology* (London: SCM, 1960); *Faith and Understanding* (London: SCM, 1969).
16. T.C. Hammond, *In Understanding be Men* (London: IVF, 1936). A similar, more recent example would be Josh McDowell, *Evidence that Demands a Verdict* (Reading: Campus Crusade, 1972).
17. Thomas J.J. Altizer and William Hamilton, *Radical Theology and the Death of God* (Indianapolis: Bobbs-Merrill, 1966).
18. Mircea Eliade, *Patterns in Comparative Religion* (New York: Sheed & Ward, 1958); see also his *Myth and Reality* (London: Allen & Unwin, 1964).

19. For a recent study of popular culture from a missiological perspective, see Craig Detweiler and Barry Taylor, *A Matrix of Meanings: finding God in Pop Culture* (Grand Rapids: Baker Academic, 2004).
20. *Ad Gentes* – see Walter Abbott (ed.), *The Documents of Vatican II* (New York: Guild, 1966), 585.
21. For a succinct introduction to the notion of 'Christendom', together with analysis of its historic significance and subsequent demise, cf. Stuart Murray, *Post-Christendom: church and mission in a strange new world* (Carlisle: Authentic Media, 2004); also David Smith, *Mission After Christendom* (London: Darton, Longman & Todd, 2003).
22. Cf. Walter Martin, *The Kingdom of the Cults* (Minneapolis: Bethany House Publishers, 1965).
23. Elliott Miller, *A Crash Course on the New Age Movement* (Grand Rapids: Baker, 1989), 14.
24. See John Drane, *The McDonaldization of the Church* (London: Darton, Longman & Todd, 2000), 55-84, where I identified seven discrete people groups in Western society.
25. Hexham, Rost and Morehead *Encountering New Religious Movements*, 18.
26. Philip Johnson, in *Encountering New Religious Movements*, 240.
27. John W. Morehead III, in *Encountering New Religious Movements*, 291.
28. For the issues involved here, see Marion Bowman, 'Reinventing the Celts', in *Religion* 23/1 (1993), 47-56; Ian Bradley, *Celtic Christianity: making myths and chasing dreams* (Edinburgh: Edinburgh University Press, 1999); Malcolm Chapman, *The Celts: the construction of a myth* (New York: St Martin's Press, 1992); Donald E. Meek, *The Quest for Celtic Christianity* (Edinburgh: Handsel Press, 2000).
29. The contrast drawn by John Finney, *Recovering the Past: Celtic and Roman Mission* (London: Darton, Longman & Todd, 1996); and George C. Hunter, *The Celtic Way of Evangelism: how Christianity can reach the West . . . again* (Nashville: Abingdon Press, 2000).
30. 'Patterns of evangelization in Paul and Jesus: a way forward in the Jesus-Paul debate?', in *Jesus of Nazareth: Lord and Christ. Essays on the historical Jesus and New Testament Christology presented to I. Howard Marshall on his 60th birthday*, ed. J.B. Green and M.M.B. Turner (Grand Rapids: Eerdmans, 1994), 281-96.
31. On the connections between the New Age and ancient Gnosticism, see John Drane, 'Ancient Gnosis for a new millennium: Nag Hammadi and the New Age', in *Cultural Change and Biblical Faith* (Carlisle: Paternoster Press, 2000), 36-56.
32. Some have regarded Paul's approach at Athens as a failure, and therefore not something to be adopted as any sort of model for Christian mission or ministry. As evidence for this, they point to the relatively small number of converts at Athens, and more especially to Paul's disdain for 'wisdom' as opposed to 'foolishness' expressed in 1 Corinthians 1:20-5. Since Corinth was the very next city he visited after Athens, the argument goes, this is

to be understood in an autobiographical way as an expression of regret for the approach he adopted in that city. This view, however, is to be rejected. For one thing, it does violence to the book of Acts, in which Luke was deliberately presenting accounts of missionary endeavour in different social, religious, and cultural contexts with the specific intention of showing how the gospel might be presented in different ways in a variety of circumstances. It also ignores the reality of the one thing that Paul did actually talk about in Athens, which was precisely the story of Jesus, including the resurrection which would have made no sense at all without mention of the cross as well. It also assumes that the apostles were always 'successful' in the sense that large numbers of people responded to their message. This was not the case, and by including stories of small response, as well as of persecution and hardship, Luke emphasized that occasions such as the Day of Pentecost (Acts 2:1-41) were few and far between, and his readers could expect that evangelism would generally be hard work with average results.

33. Tex Sample, *White Soul: Country Music, the Church and working Americans* (Nashville: Abingdon Press, 1996), 13, 32, 45.
34. David J. Bosch, *Transforming Mission* (Maryknoll: Orbis, 1991).
35. John Drane, Ross Clifford and Philip Johnson, *Beyond Prediction: the Tarot and Your Spirituality* (Oxford: Lion, 2001).
36. For recent affirmation of this approach, see *The Thailand Report on Religious and non-religious Spirituality* (San Clemente: LCWE, 2005), a Lausanne Occasional Paper reporting the 2004 Consultation on World Evangelisation; and Yvonne Richmond *et al.*, *Evangelism in a Spiritual Age* (London: Church House Publishing, 2005). For case studies and specific examples of such ministry, Ross Clifford and Philip Johnson, *Jesus and the Gods of the New Age* (Oxford: Lion, 2001).
37. Philip Johnson and John Smulo, in *Encountering New Religious Movements*, 224.

Chapter 4: Creating Churches for Spiritual Searchers

1. Cf. General Synod of the Church of England, *Mission-Shaped Church* (London: Church House Publishing, 2004).
2. Cf. David B. Barrett, George T. Kurian and Todd M. Johnson, *World Christian Encyclopedia*, 2nd edn in two volumes (Oxford: Oxford University Press, 2001); and annual updates in the first issue of each year of *International Bulletin of Missionary Research*. For a scholarly analysis of what this might mean, see Philip Jenkins, *The Next Christendom: the coming of Global Christianity* (Oxford: Oxford University Press, 2002).
3. For further reflections on this, see John Drane and Olive Fleming Drane, *Family Fortunes: Faith-full caring for today's families* (London: Darton, Longman & Todd, 2004).
4. Lee Pelham Cotton, 'Kneel and Kiss the Ground', in *SageWoman* 64 (2004), 7.

5. Alan Jamieson, *A Churchless Faith: Faith journeys beyond the Churches* (London: SPCK, 2002); William D. Hendricks, *Exit Interviews* (Chicago: Moody Press, 1993); Philip J. Richter and Leslie J. Francis, *Gone but not Forgotten: Church leaving and returning* (London: Darton, Longman & Todd, 1998). Cf. also Michael J. Fanstone, *The Sheep that Got Away* (London: Monarch, 1993); Michael Moynagh, *Changing World, Changing Church* (London: Monarch, 2001), 7-81; John Drane, *The McDonaldization of the Church* (London: Darton, Longman & Todd, 2000), 34-84.
6. Cf. Alan Jamieson, *A Churchless Faith* for many specific examples of individuals who fall into this category.
7. George Ritzer, *The McDonaldization of Society* (Thousand Oaks: Pine Forge Press, 1993), 26.
8. See John Drane, *The McDonaldization of the Church* (London: Darton, Longman & Todd, 2000), 34-54; and George Ritzer, *McDonaldization: the Reader* (Thousand Oaks: Pine Forge Press, 2002), 151-7.
9. Shirley Maclaine, *Out on a Limb* (London: Bantam, 1986), 198.
10. http://www.beliefnet.com/story/67/story_6758_4.html.
11. Drane, *The McDonaldization of the Church*, 55-84.
12. Cf. George Ritzer, *McDonaldization: The Reader*, 71, 151-7.
13. John Wolffe, in *Church Times*, 9 March 2001, 16.
14. Leslie J. Francis, *Faith and Psychology: personality, religion and the individual* (London: Darton, Longman & Todd, 2005).
15. Charlotte L. Craig, *Psychological Types of Churchgoers in the United Kingdom: an empirical analysis*, unpublished Ph.D. dissertation, University of Wales, Bangor (2005).
16. Charlotte Craig, 'Knowing your Congregation', *Country Way* 37 (autumn 2004), 25.
17. For the norms, cf. Elizabeth Kendall, *The Myers Briggs type indicator manual: UK supplement* (Oxford: Oxford Psychologists Press, 1998).
18. For further historical reflections on some of the reasons for this, see John Drane, 'From Creeds to Burgers: religious control, spiritual search, and the future of the world', in James R. Beckford and John Walliss, *Religion and Social Theory* (London: Ashgate, forthcoming 2005); also in George Ritzer, *McDonaldization: the Reader*, 2nd edn (Thousand Oaks: Sage, forthcoming 2005).
19. John Drane, *Faith in a Changing Culture* (London: HarperCollins, 1997), 218-23; cf. Richard V. Peace, *Conversion in the New Testament* (Grand Rapids: Eerdmans, 1999).
20. Seyoon Kim, *The Origin of Paul's Gospel* (Grand Rapids: Eerdmans, 1984).
21. For this in a context of practical theology, see Don Browning, *A Fundamental Practical Theology: Descriptive and Strategic Proposals* (Minneapolis: Fortress Press, 1991); James Woodward and Stephen Pattison (eds.), *The Blackwell Reader in Pastoral and Practical Theology* (Oxford: Blackwell, 1999). The concept is of course also central to Liberation Theology: cf. Robert McAfee Brown, *Liberation Theology: An*

Introductory Guide (Louisville: Westminster John Knox Press, 1993); Christopher Rowland (ed.), *The Cambridge Companion to Liberation Theology* (Cambridge: Cambridge University Press, 1999).

22. Leith Anderson, *A Church for the Twenty-First Century* (Minneapolis: Bethany House, 1992), 21.
23. W.F. Storrar, 'From Braveheart to Faint-heart: worship and culture in post-modern Scotland', in B.D. Spinks and I.R. Torrance (eds.), *To Glorify God: Essays on Modern Reformed Liturgy* (Edinburgh: T & T Clark, 1999), 78; for more on this cf. John Drane, *Cultural Change and Biblical Faith* (Carlisle: Paternoster Press, 2000), 112-16.
24. Paul Heelas and Linda Woodhead, *The Spiritual Revolution* (Oxford: Blackwell, 2005), 30.
25. Bhagwan Shree Rajneesh, *I am the Gate* (New York: Harper & Row, 1977), 18.
26. And the trend shows no signs of abating, with a constant stream of popular publications claiming to rewrite early Christian history, the most recent example being Dan Brown, *The DaVinci Code* (New York: Doubleday, 2003).
27. Maclaine, *Out on a Limb*, 210.
28. *ibid.*, 215.
29. Donal Dorr, *Time for a Change* (Dublin: Columba Press, 2004), 197.
30. Cf. Peter Brierley (ed.), *UK Christian Handbook Religious Trends 4* (London: Christian Research, 2003).
31. Heelas and Woodhead, *Spiritual Revolution*, 148.
32. *ibid.*, 88.
33. *ibid.*, 99.
34. John Drane, *The McDonaldization of the Church*, 173-82; Grace Jantzen, 'Necrophilia and Natality: what does it mean to be religious?' in *Scottish Journal of Religious Studies* 19/1 (1998), 101-21; Margaret L. Hammer, *Giving Birth: Reclaiming Biblical Metaphor for Pastoral Practice* (Louisville: Westminster John Knox Press, 1994).
35. Dorr, *Time for a Change*, 47.
36. Douglas Coupland, *Microserfs* (London: Flamingo, 1995), 313.
37. Something that can be documented from the rise in single person homes. The 2001 UK census showed that 32% of homes are occupied by single people, representing 25% of the population – with projections that in ten years or less 40% of homes will be occupied by single people, comprising more than 50% of the population. The 2000 US census highlighted the same trend, with more than 40% of all adult Americans being single, and the traditional family of two married parents and their biologically related children accounting for only 23.5% of all households.
38. Sheryl Garratt, *Adventures in Wonderland: a Decade of Club Culture* (London: Headline, 1998), 305.
39. Faithless, *Sunday 8pm* (London: Cheeky Records, 1998).
40. For more on this, cf. John Drane, 'Contemporary culture and the reinven-

tion of sacramental spirituality' in Geoffrey Rowell and Christine Hall (eds.), *The Gestures of God* (London: Continuum, 2004), 37-55.

41. Marion Leach Jacobsen, *Crowded Pews and Lonely People* (Wheaton: Tyndale House, 1975).
42. Heelas and Woodhead, *Spiritual Revolution*, 105.
43. Ian Wray, 'Buddhism and Psychotherapy', in G. Claxton, *Beyond Therapy* (London: Wisdom Publications, 1986), 160-1.
44. Maclaine, *Out on a Limb*, 136.
45. J.L. Simmons, *The Emerging New Age* (Santa Fe: Bear & Co., 1990), 69-70.
46. The classic work here is Matthew Fox, *Original Blessing* (Santa Fe: Bear & Co., 1983). See also his article 'Spirituality for a New Era', in Duncan S. Ferguson (ed.), *New Age Spirituality* (Louisville: Westminster/John Knox Press, 1993), 196-219. Fox has been rightly criticized for his simplistic rewriting of Christian history, and there is no question that the answers he gives to his own questions are quite unsatisfactory. But the questions remain, and will need to be addressed.
47. Bryant Myers, 'Another look at "Holistic Mission"', in *Evangelical Missions Quarterly* 35 (1999), 286.
48. Dorr, *Time for a Change*, 122.
49. *ibid.*, 198.
50. While there is of course some evidence connecting Western missionary movements with imperialist expansion, the specific causal relationship between the two is often exaggerated. For a necessary correction, see Brian Stanley, *The Bible and the Flag: Protestant missions and British imperialism in the nineteenth and twentieth centuries* (Leicester: Apollos, 1990); Lamin Sanneh, *Encountering the West: Christianity and the Global Cultural Process* (London: HarperCollins, 1993); Brian Stanley, *Christian Missions and the Enlightenment* (Grand Rapids: Eerdmans, 2001).
51. For detailed examination of all these issues in relation to the Bible, see Aida Besançon Spencer *et al.*, *The Goddess Revival* (Grand Rapids: Baker, 1995).
52. R. Ackoff, *Creating the Corporate Future* (New York: Wiley, 1981), 26.
53. *ibid.*, 44.
54. For specific examples of this in the Gospels, see my *Faith in a Changing Culture*, 82-107, 218-23.
55. Cf. Olive M. Fleming Drane, *Clowns, Storytellers, Disciples* (Oxford: BRF, 2000).
56. David Hay and Kate Hunt, *Understanding the Spirituality of People who don't go to Church* (Nottingham: University of Nottingham Centre for the Study of Human Relations, 2000).
57. At the time of writing, it is envisaged that this will be published by Darton, Longman & Todd during 2006, under the title *After McDonaldization: how not to be Church.*
58. François Lyotard, *The Postmodern Condition* (Minneapolis: University of Minnesota Press, 1993), xxiv.

59. See, among many others, Stanley J. Grenz, *A Primer on Postmodernism* (Grand Rapids: Eerdmans, 1996); Douglas Groothuis, *Truth Decay* (Downers Grove: InterVarsity, 2000).
60. For an ongoing discussion of his new opinions, see http://www.secweb.org/asset.asp?AssetID=369. Whatever his new position turns out to be, it is obviously not as militantly atheistic as that proposed in his book *God and Philosophy* (London: Hutchinson, 1966).
61. Cf. Alister McGrath, *The Twilight of Atheism: the rise and fall of disbelief in the modern world* (London: Rider, 2004).
62. Heelas and Woodhead, *Spiritual Revolution*, 148.
63. Jeremy Carrette and Richard King, *Selling Spirituality* (London: Routledge, 2004), 68.
64. *ibid.*, 5.
65. *ibid.*, 179.
66. *ibid.*, 3.
67. Raymond Fung, *The Isaiah Vision* (Geneva: WCC, 1992).
68. *Mission and Evangelism, an Ecumenical Affirmation* (Geneva: WCC, 1982), paragraph 28.
69. The most recent statistics show that the number of Christian martyrs is currently running at the rate of 169,000 per annum, and continues to increase. Cf. David B. Barrett, Todd M. Johnson and Peter F. Crossing, 'Missiometrics 2005: a global survey of world mission', in *International Bulletin of Missionary Research* 29/1 (2005), 29.
70. Heelas and Woodhead, *Spiritual Revolution*, 147.
71. Laurie Beth Jones, *Jesus, Entrepreneur* (New York: Three Rivers Press, 2001), 251-2.

Index

Subjects

People